Wild INDIA

The wildlife and scenery of India and Nepal

"संकल्प"

यह स्वीकार करते हुए कि प्राकृतिक वातावरण की रक्षा का मौलिक महत्व है, जिस पर मानव संस्कृति आधारित है, मैं यह सत्यनिष्ठ प्रतिज्ञा करता हूँ कि मैं, लगातार समाप्त हो रहे वन्य प्राणियों और निरन्तर कम हो रहे वन क्षेत्रों कि रक्षा के लिये भरसक प्रयत्न करुँगा, जो कि हमारी भावी पीढ़ियों के धरोहर के रूप में है।

PLEDGE

Convinced of the Fundamental Importance of Conserving the Natural Environment, upon which Rests the foundation of human Civilization, I Solemnly Pledge that I will Spare no Efforts to preserve our Vanishing wild Life and our dwindling forest areas which our Generation Holds in trust for Posterity.

वन्यजन्तु परिरक्षण संगठन जोशीमठ

Wild INDIA

The wildlife and scenery of India and Nepal

Collins
Grafton Street, London.

This book is dedicated to the memory of
Shrimati Indira Gandhi, who throughout
her long service as Prime Minister of India
set a shining example to the world by her
determination to protect the rich heritage of
her country's wildlife. Her personal interest
in the production of this book was an
inspiration to the authors.

Foreword by HRH The Duke of Edinburgh KT, KG

Anyone concerned with the conservation of nature tends to be obsessed with the disasters. There are plenty of conservation disaster stories in India but, as this splendid book demonstrates so beautifully, there are many success stories and much of her superb natural heritage still survives.

I am sure that **Wild India** *will give a great deal of pleasure for its own sake but if ever a case had to be made for the conservation of the world's natural heritage, it will be found most persuasively in the pictures and text of this book.*

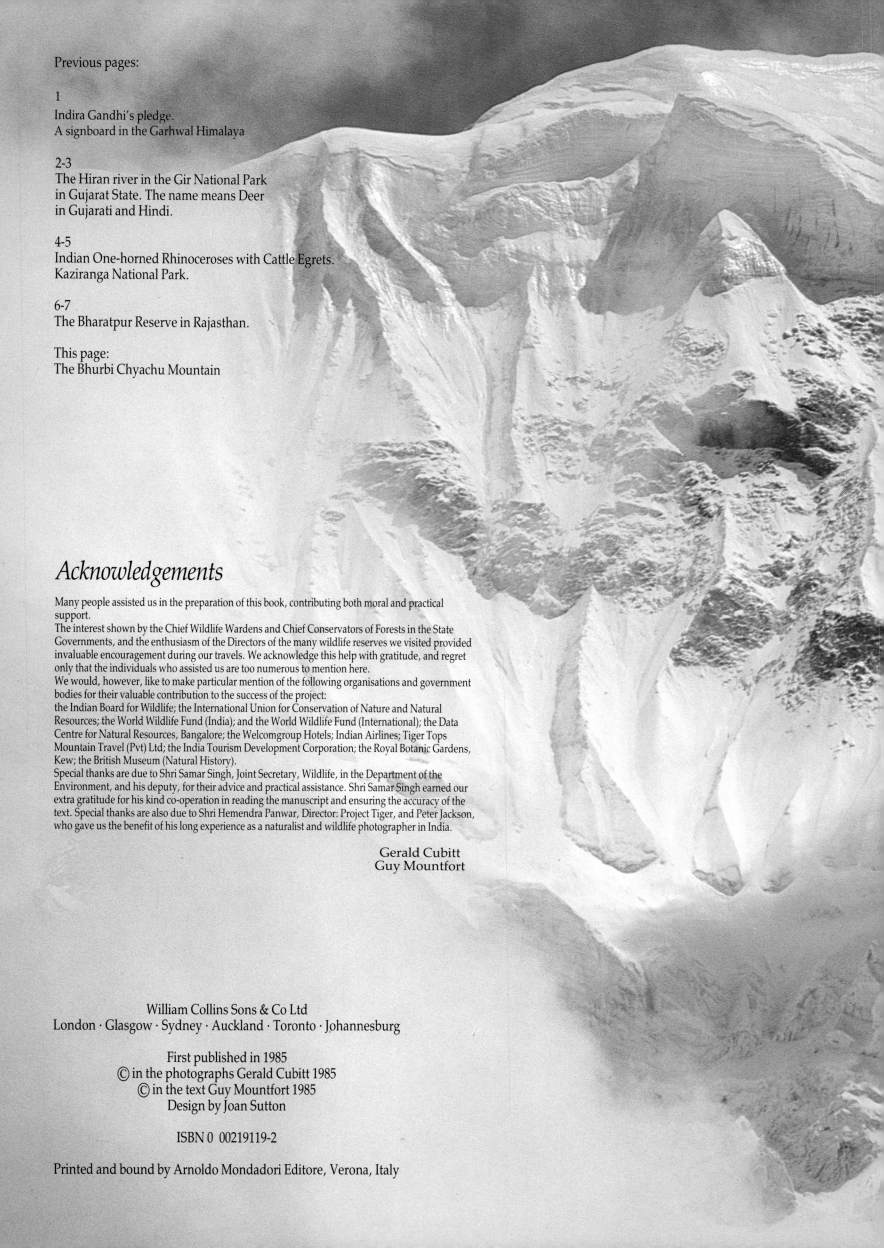

Previous pages:

1
Indira Gandhi's pledge.
A signboard in the Garhwal Himalaya

2-3
The Hiran river in the Gir National Park
in Gujarat State. The name means Deer
in Gujarati and Hindi.

4-5
Indian One-horned Rhinoceroses with Cattle Egrets.
Kaziranga National Park.

6-7
The Bharatpur Reserve in Rajasthan.

This page:
The Bhurbi Chyachu Mountain

Acknowledgements

Many people assisted us in the preparation of this book, contributing both moral and practical support.
The interest shown by the Chief Wildlife Wardens and Chief Conservators of Forests in the State Governments, and the enthusiasm of the Directors of the many wildlife reserves we visited provided invaluable encouragement during our travels. We acknowledge this help with gratitude, and regret only that the individuals who assisted us are too numerous to mention here.
We would, however, like to make particular mention of the following organisations and government bodies for their valuable contribution to the success of the project:
the Indian Board for Wildlife; the International Union for Conservation of Nature and Natural Resources; the World Wildlife Fund (India); and the World Wildlife Fund (International); the Data Centre for Natural Resources, Bangalore; the Welcomgroup Hotels; Indian Airlines; Tiger Tops Mountain Travel (Pvt) Ltd; the India Tourism Development Corporation; the Royal Botanic Gardens, Kew; the British Museum (Natural History).
Special thanks are due to Shri Samar Singh, Joint Secretary, Wildlife, in the Department of the Environment, and his deputy, for their advice and practical assistance. Shri Samar Singh earned our extra gratitude for his kind co-operation in reading the manuscript and ensuring the accuracy of the text. Special thanks are also due to Shri Hemendra Panwar, Director: Project Tiger, and Peter Jackson, who gave us the benefit of his long experience as a naturalist and wildlife photographer in India.

Gerald Cubitt
Guy Mountfort

William Collins Sons & Co Ltd
London · Glasgow · Sydney · Auckland · Toronto · Johannesburg

First published in 1985
© in the photographs Gerald Cubitt 1985
© in the text Guy Mountfort 1985
Design by Joan Sutton

ISBN 0 00219119-2

Printed and bound by Arnoldo Mondadori Editore, Verona, Italy

Contents

Introduction

A traveller arriving by air almost invariably lands in the small hours of the night. When the doors open, a gust of heat like the blast from a furnace reminds him that this is India. The last time I landed at Dum-Dum, Calcutta's airport, at 2 a.m. the temperature stood at a clammy 33°C. In spite of the hour, the airport was swarming with people and every bench crowded to capacity with shrouded, sleeping figures and their cloth-bound bundles. Many lay untidily on the floor, still wearing their tinsel garlands of departure, but looking like the aftermath of a massacre. Airports in India, like railway stations, serve as neighbourhood dormitories, through which travellers must fight their way, aided by the enthusiastic khaki-clad baggage touts, who perhaps an hour later will triumphantly find their suitcases for them and obtain a taxi. Seasoned travellers will know that it is useless to hurry and that one after another the many officials, with contemplative devotion to duty, will examine minutely every stamp on every page of every passport. In planning an itinerary they will also have learned to accept at face value the charmingly worded notice stamped on the Indian Tourist Department brochure that 'all factual information is liable to change without notice.' What could be more disarmingly frank than this?

Whether you spend the remainder of the night in a modern hotel or in a mahogany and red velvet relic of the Victorian era, the unmistakable smell and sounds of India will greet the new day. The smell is compounded of burning cow-dung, spices and hot dust. From the roof-tops will come the squealing of Black Kites, locally called Pariahs for their scavenging habits, and as likely as not you will hear the chatter of the ubiquitous Mynahs. In the streets below there will be the incessant noise of taxi-horns and of people. Hundreds, thousands of them, some hurrying to work, others wandering aimlessly or talking in animated groups, or begging. In India it is almost impossible to escape the sight of people. In 1984 her population was approaching 750,000,000 and increasing at a rate of 1,000,000 a month. The city of Calcutta alone has a population of 10,500,000 — an average density of nearly 100,000 people to the square kilometre.

You can generalise about some countries, but not about India. It is a land of too many superlatives and contrasts, too great a range of widely differing scenes, too bewildering a complexity of ethnic origins, traditions, languages and religions. It is an unbelievably beautiful land, whether seen in the glare of the midday sun when its colours are harshly brilliant, or at dawn when the palm trees stand like disembodied sentinels above the candescent mist rising from the paddyfields. Wherever you go, its colourful pageant flows past you, ever changing.

This fascinating region is so vast and its life so diverse that no-one can know more than a fraction of it. In offering the reader something of the impression which it has made on me I am aware that it has been acquired, perhaps imperfectly, through Western eyes. The many photographs that follow, however beautiful in themselves, can represent only a fraction of the splendour which at every turn awaits the traveller. Because my interest and that of my colleague, the photographer Gerald Cubitt, lies primarily in the natural environment, we have deliberately omitted the incredibly rich heritage of man-made treasures, such as the voluptuous Hindu and assertively austere Islamic shrines, which for 3000 years have continued to increase in number. These are described and illustrated in a host of guide-books.

The India of the British Raj embraced not only the great Indian peninsula and its many princely States, but also what is now Pakistan to the west, Nepal, Sikkim and Bhutan to the north and what has now become Bangladesh in the east. Ceylon (now called Sri Lanka) and even Burma, which has nothing in common with India, were usually included, if only because they were coloured pink on the map as being at that time within the British sphere of political influence. Since the Partition of India in 1947 all these countries have gained their independence as Sovereign States, except Sikkim — which has become part of India.

Although this book deals principally with India, the phrase 'Indian subcontinent' is used when reference to these adjoining countries is also involved, for example in the case of the distribution of animal species or geological features. Sri Lanka is omitted because this great island has been separated from the continental land-mass for many millions of years.

Visitors to India may be confused by the disappearance of once familiar place-names, because in 1956 the States were reorganized and many were given new names. India itself has the Hindi name Bharat, and although English is still the *lingua franca* of nearly all educated Indians, Hindi is officially the national language under the Constitution of India. However, since each ethnic group fiercely demands that its language should remain inviolate, it may be some years before this becomes fully effective. There would be an obvious unifying advantage in a single language. At present there are 15 'official' languages and 45 others spoken to a lesser degree. In addition, more than 700 quite different dialects are still current in various parts of the country. If ever a government had difficulty in communicating its policies to its people, it is that of India.

A crowded scene in Old Delhi. With a population of some 750 million, India is enduring severe social and economic problems related to ever-growing human pressures.

The Legacies of Invasion

To understand the reasons for the extraordinary diversity of the Indian scene one must turn to its turbulent history and to the complex influences of its numerous religions. For 3000 years the renown of the rich natural resources of the subcontinent attracted powerful invaders, many of whom brought with them new religious beliefs which they established during their conquests. Indians often proudly claim to belong to the world's oldest civilization. It is certainly a very ancient one, though historical records before the Aryan invasion are vague. It probably dates back to the middle of the third millennium BC. Traces of Palaeolithic man exist, but evidence indicating a sequence of culture is lacking. The most important finds were made during excavations of the Bronze Age cities of Harappa and Mohenjo-Daro in the Indus valley. These suggest an occupation of about 600 years between 2500 and 1900 BC, by an agrarian Dravidian people – probably from Iran. Their strange pictographic alphabet and seals reveal a skilful craftsmanship superior to that of the Indo-Aryans. From their seals and figurines we learn that Tigers, Elephants and One-horned Rhinoceroses lived in the valley of the Indus, where today there is almost treeless desert. As no weapons were discovered in the excavations, these peaceable people were probably exterminated by a more warlike tribe.

The first large-scale invasion of which records survive was that of the Aryans, who are thought to have come from Russia. By 600 BC they had occupied all of northern India, with a capital near the present location of Delhi. Hinduism was already established, and here the Brahmins evolved classical Sanskrit. New religions were introduced with the teachings of Buddha and Mahavira. By the time of Alexander's short-lived invasion in 327 BC, northern India was ruled by the Mauryas, while the south was in disarray under the rule of Nanda, a usurper who had briefly seized most of the peninsular region. The rise of Emperor Ashoka in 274 BC saw the establishment of Buddhism throughout all of India except the extreme south. Ashoka was the world's first known conservationist, and his Fifth Edict, protecting all wildlife except certain animals required for food, can still be read on the stone pillars which he erected on the boundaries of his empire. After his death, Buddhism began to decline and the Hindu religion to expand again, while India broke up into a number of small kingdoms.

Invasion by the Greeks, the Sakas, the Parthians and the Kushans followed in succession and these further enriched Indian culture. The Kushans did much to restore Buddhism. The third century AD witnessed a blossoming of the creative arts during the Gupta era, which was the golden age of Sanskrit literature, art, architecture, science and philosophy. But because of confusing dynastic rivalries during the following four centuries, India once more became fragmented and unable to resist invasion by the White Huns and the powerful Arab legions. The subsequent long Moslem era was marked by much ruthless slaughter and pillage, which again changed the face of the country. By the beginning of the 16th century the Islamic faith had replaced Hinduism over a great part of India, although this religion remained dominant.

The Moghul emperors who next ruled India were descendants of the Mongol Genghiz Khan. A distant relative, Tamerlane (who enjoyed hunting rhinoceroses in Kashmir), tried unsuccessfully to suppress Hinduism, sacking Delhi and massacring 100,000 people. The greatest of the Moghuls was undoubtedly Akbar, who ruled from 1556 to 1605. His administration was skilful and his treatment of Hindus conciliatory. Unhappily, his successor Jahengir was not interested in administration and his extravagance speedily undid most of his father's reforms. Shah Jehan, who followed him, introduced another period of literary progress and a programme of magnificent building, culminating in the treasured Taj Mahal at Agra as a monument to his widow, who had presented him with no fewer than 14 children. But the fabulous splendour of the Moghul court and the Peacock Throne brought India to bankruptcy and the empire began to collapse. Shah Jehan's successor, Aurangzeb (1658-

1707), was a cruel religious bigot who persecuted the Hindus and by savage taxation of the peasants finally ruined the economy completely. The opportunity for another attempted take-over was quickly seized, first by Persians again, then by the Afghans and finally by the Marathas, who held power until 1761.

Meanwhile, covetous Western eyes had been turned towards the riches of India. First in the field were the Portuguese, who gained control of the Malabar coast. Next came the Dutch and the British and after them the French, the Danes and the Swedes. Yet another religion, Christianity, was introduced to the bewildered Indians. All the Western trading enterprises made treaties with various local Princes and fought each other in the scramble for advantage. Thanks to the power of its navy, Britain succeeded in excluding its competitors, and after many vicissitudes India became part of the British Empire in 1886. After the second World War, in which 2,000,000 Indian soldiers played a conspicuous part in all theatres, India finally gained independence in 1947 and proudly became a self-governing Republic. As Hindus and Moslems remained politically irreconcilable, Pakistan emerged as a separate Moslem nation. More recent history saw the transition of East Pakistan into independent Bangladesh.

Whatever the rights or wrongs of the long period of the British Raj, it bequeathed a legacy of lasting value in the form of an efficient civil service and a unifying network of roads and railways, to say nothing of a highly skilled forestry service and many hospitals, schools and grandiose pseudo-Gothic civic buildings which still stand incongruously in Indian cities. Slavery, female infanticide and *suttee* (the burning of widows on their husbands' funeral pyres) had been firmly abolished.

The main religions of India, in numerical order of importance, are now those of the Hindus (of which there are 45,000,000), the Moslems, the Christians, the Sikhs, the Jains, the Buddhists and the Zoroastrians, the last-mentioned being chiefly Parsees and Iranians. Within these sometimes strangely intermixed religions are many differing sects — particularly among Hindus, to whom religion is part of everyday life. The bewildering Pantheon of Hindu gods and demons, many of which have alternative names, are worshipped at different times. Broadly speaking, they ensure reward for virtue in the next incarnation — and punishment for ill-doing. To a Hindu, God and Nature are one. No Hindu will willingly harm any animal, and the cow is regarded as sacred, as are certain other animals.

There is a considerable measure of animism in the more primitive forms of Hinduism. In Vedic theology all aspects of Nature have their own deities; thus Vayu rules the wind, Soma the plants, Garuda the birds, Jambavan the bears and so on. The elephant-headed, four-armed and pot-bellied god Ganesa must be propitiated before any important undertaking. The mythical Nagas, represented by a many-headed cobra, are the guardians of the underworld. All the Hindu poets and legends stress the moral imperative to regard Nature as beneficial to man.

The Jains are dissenters from Hinduism, and in its extreme form Jainism is a monastic order eschewing all material possessions. A strict Jain will kill no living thing and must keep his mouth covered in case his breath pollutes the air or harms flies. Moslems, on the other hand, safe in the knowledge that the Koran extolls the virtues of the chase, are usually keen and skilful hunters. The fact that Hindus and Jains between them represent the great majority of the Indian population has undoubtedly been a major factor in maintaining the richness of Indian wildlife.

Geography and Climate

The roughly triangular Indian subcontinent is more than 3000 kilometres wide in the north and of similar length from the Himalayas to Cape Comorin, giving a total area of nearly 5,000,000 square kilometres, or roughly the size of Europe west of the USSR. It has three well defined geographical regions – the Himalayan, the alluvial Indo-Gangetic Plain and the southern tableland of the Deccan. Each differs widely in appearance, languages and traditions.

It is generally recognised now that peninsular India was once part of the super-continent Gondwanaland, which included Africa, Antarctica, Madagascar, Australia and South America. Evidence of the link includes the remains of a primitive lizard, *Lystrosaurus*, found in South Africa, Antarctica, Bengal and China. As Gondwanaland broke up, India became separated and drifted across the globe on its molten crust, to crash slowly, but with titanic force, into Eurasia 40-60 million years ago. It extinguished the ancient Tethys Ocean, whose bed has been thrust up to 4000 metres in Tibet along the suture line of the Indian and Eurasian plates, just south of the Yarlung Zangbo river. Fossilized sea-shells such as ammonites can be seen here embedded in the sandstone and limestone rocks. These are now 800 kilometres from the nearest sea and 4 kilometres above the present sea level. The Indian plate has continued to thrust under Eurasia, and the Himalayas, which have risen in several great upheavals, are still rising at a rate of about a centimetre a year and moving northward at five centimetres a year. The great height reached by the range in the late Pleistocene created a weather barrier which is responsible for India's monsoon climate.

The climate of the subcontinent is described as tropical monsoon, but it varies greatly and can offer extremes of heat and cold, total drought and torrential rain. In some areas not a drop of rain will fall for two years or more. Other regions may suddenly receive two years of average rainfall in only two days. Factors controlling these vagaries are the mountain ranges, the vastness of the exposed plain – extending for 2250 kilometres between the Indus and the Brahmaputra – and the extent of the long coastlines, which are exposed to the full force of the wind from both the Arabian Sea and the Indian Ocean. The western region – Pakistan, the Ranns of Kutch and the Rajasthan Desert – are dry and witheringly hot, the monsoon clouds passing over them but rarely releasing rain. In the east, monsoon rain is frequent, with an astonishing record of 10.87 metres one year in the Khasi Hills. In the alluvial plain of the Ganges and Brahmaputra the monsoon rains pass regularly back and forth, depositing more than 2.5 metres of water a year. India's capital, Delhi, gets a mere 73 centimetres or so, comparable to rainfall in England, but mainly between June and October. The peninsular region north of the Vindhya range has a fairly copious rainfall, while the plateau to the south usually receives its rain a month

later. Cyclones accompanied by tidal waves periodically devastate the coasts of the Bay of Bengal, with horrifying loss of life. In 1970 about 200,000 people were drowned when a cyclone hit the Sundarbans region in Bangladesh. But in general terms one might say that Indian weather is cool in January and February and hot from March to May, with the monsoon advancing from June to October and retreating again in November and December. The first quarter of the year is usually delightful, with brilliant sunshine and only modest heat recalling a Mediterranean summer.

Vegetation and the Monsoon

The subcontinent is extremely rich in plant species, no fewer than 45,000 having been identified. However, by comparison with some other major regions it is somewhat lacking in endemic tree species. It makes up for this by the large number originating in the surrounding countries. European and Siberian origins are obvious in the coniferous trees of the Himalayas. In the western half are Deodars, Long-leafed Pines, Western Himalayan Firs and Bhutan Cypresses. In the more tropical eastern half these are replaced by other local varieties of Spruce, Larch, Hemlock, Pine and Fir. The thorny xerophytic vegetation of the Pakistan and Rajasthan deserts much resembles that of Arabia and the Middle East, while that of the southern peninsula has fairly obvious Malaysian affinities, with a smaller admixture of East African.

In the humid Gangetic Plain the native Sal forests are the mainstay of the timber industry. Teak, the most important quick-growing commercial species, is cultivated chiefly in areas of high

Seasonal changes from the dry season to the wet season produce very pronounced results, as shown by these views of a lake in the Ranthambhor Tiger Reserve.

rainfall in the east and south. The commercial crops of the subcontinent are rice and other cereals, tea, coffee, sugar cane, rubber, cotton, jute, oilseed and an abundance of fruits, nuts and spices. Further variety in the vegetation has resulted from countless deliberate introductions from other continents. Including these, the number of tree species alone is now about 1200, many of which have spectacular blossoms and have become naturalised in the wild.

The most common and one of the most beautiful Indian trees is the Cassia, or Indian Laburnum, which produces masses of drooping bunches of yellow flowers, followed by dangling seed-pods 60 centimetres long. In coastal regions the Indian Coral Tree is equally colourful, with spikes of bright coral-red flowers. Because of its hard wood it is frequently used for fencing, and when the wood is fresh the posts readily take root to produce new wayside trees. Many city streets are lined with Queen's Flower, the purple blossoms of which fall to carpet the pavements. Another widespread species is the Shisham, which has clusters of white flowers and, unlike many other Indian trees, maintains some of its leaves throughout the year.

One of the introduced species is the Baobab, which has a grotesque bulbous trunk and was brought in from Africa many centuries ago by Moslem traders. The Gulmohar (Flamboyant) came from Madagascar and is now perhaps the most common garden tree. Its abundant orange-red flowers, produced in February when it is bare of leaves, and its later feathery foliage brighten many a city park, as do the scarlet bells of the Tulip Tree. The various Eucalypts came from Australia and Tasmania, the Sandalwood from Indonesia, while the Jacarandas, with their beautiful lilac-blue flowers, originated in Brazil.

The Flame of the Forest, which flowers at the beginning of the hot season, is another widespread and spectacular species, with orange-red blossoms. The extravagantly-flowering Silk Cotton was known in the earliest Indian mythology as the tree beneath which Pitamaha, the creator of the world, rested after his labours. It is one of the best shade-trees and produces large red flowers, the calyx of which is eaten as a delicacy. The cotton dropping from its fat seed-pods blankets the surroundings, and is harvested for stuffing mattresses. Its timber is valuable and its gum is used medicinally. The sharp conical spines on its bark deter anyone from climbing it, but despite this, a friend of mine was once obliged to climb a Silk Cotton at high speed when treed by a Tigress, only to find that it housed a colony of savagely biting tree-ants, to which he had to submit for half an hour before the Tigress withdrew.

My favourites among the flowering trees are the various Bauhinias, with their large mauve, pink or white single blossoms. The Climbing Bauhinias are almost as beautiful, their masses of creamy-white flowers cascading down from hundreds of great trees in the foothills of the Himalayas and in the forests of the Western Ghats.

Two trees have important religious significance in India. One, indigenous in the sub-Himalayan region, is the Banyan; the other is the Peepal. Both members of the numerous fig family, these trees are characterised by powerful and invasive growth. If planted near buildings, they easily demolish them. They are very long-lived. The Banyan increases by roots descending from the branches, so that they spread over an astonishingly large area. A venerable tree of this species in Maharashtra is said to hold the record with a breadth of nearly 200 metres and a circumference of 577 metres; the official record, however, is held by an immense Banyan in the Botanic Gardens at Calcutta. Villagers venerate both species and make use of the extensive shelter they provide as community centres. The Buddha is said to have achieved enlightenment while meditating under a Peepal, and both Hindus and Buddhists hold religious ceremonies beneath these trees, which they often believe to be female Banyans. One such tree is said to be 2150 years old, although the evidence for this is somewhat doubtful.

Among the most frequently seen palm trees are the Palmyra or Toddy Palm, the Coconut, the Sago, the Wild Date and the Betel Nut. The red, expectorated juice of chewed Betel Nut stains the ground in every Indian town and village. According to Indian doctors, the juice is one of the major causes of mouth cancer. In the Mangrove swamps the channels are often fringed with graceful, short-stemmed Nipa Palms, which are the mainstay of the Bengali thatching industry.

Botanists divide the vegetation of the subcontinent into 15 distinct climatic zones, ranging from tropical wet evergreen, semi-evergreen and moist deciduous to dry temperate, tidal and alpine. Each has distinctive communities of dependent wildlife. The vegetation and indeed all forms of life, including man, are governed by the power and vagaries of the monsoon. The rains are seldom predictable. In some years and in some regions the monsoon capriciously fails, and there is widespread drought and famine. Wells run dry over huge areas and, where water remains, it is measured by the half-cupful. The lesson of the imbalance of Nature is a harsh one. Equally capriciously, the volume of monsoon rainfall in India may be so great that rivers rise by as much as 32 metres, drowning hundreds of villages and causing great tracts of soil and vegetation, including large trees, to slide down mountain slopes and demolish

roads and railways. Despite dams and barrages, such catastrophes are frequent, and the loss of life is horrific. In 1983 more than 800 people were drowned in Gujarat State alone, while 1000 were drowned elsewhere in India. Every year, hundreds of millions of tons of valuable top-soil are carried down the rivers and into the sea, where new islands are created by the accumulated silt. One such island appeared off the mouth of the Ganges a few years ago, and is already more than 16 kilometres wide. Charts are of little value near the river mouth because of the constantly changing contours of the sea floor caused by the discharge of silt.

The sheer violence and duration of monsoon rainfall as experienced in north-east India and Burma has to be seen to be believed. The most torrential European rain is by comparison a mere shower. Nevertheless, it is the life-blood of the subcontinent. When the monsoon breaks, the villagers rejoice and give thanks to the god Varuna, the controller of the waters of life. The starving domestic buffaloes run bellowing to the village ponds, which for months have been mere sun-cracked depressions, to wallow with only their eyes and noses above the longed-for water. Were it not for the cushioning effect of the dense forests in the mountains and hills, the north-eastern parts of India would long since have lost most of their essential top-soil. There is clear evidence of this in areas which have been clear-felled to make way for the expansion of human settlements; instead of rich and varied forest there is now a semi-desert of exposed laterite subsoil.

Both vegetation and bird life in India are largely controlled by the incidence of the monsoon. Many trees and plants which provide fruit bear crops twice a year in conformity with the monsoon cycle. The migration and nesting of most birds also conform, so that advantage can be taken of the explosive abundance of insect life and fresh vegetation which follows. Certain migratory birds are regarded by farmers as infallible heralds of the rain – for example, the Rain Quail, the Koel and other hawk-cuckoos, and the Yellow Wagtail. Western farmers may smile at this, but in India the accuracy of the movement of migratory birds in relation to the rains and the abundance of food is not to be scoffed at.

Three regions are world famous among botanists – Kashmir, Nepal and Bhutan. The higher reaches of Kashmir and the Nepalese Himalayas provided many of the most beautiful alpine flowers which now grow in our gardens, while from Bhutan and Sikkim originated a large percentage of our cultivated orchids and greenhouse plants. For Rhododendrons and Azaleas, the area between the Khumbu and Mount Kanchengjunga on the border of Sikkim offers the opportunity to see a truly staggering variety of species and such a combination of massed colours as to render anyone speechless.

In Sikkim, Bhutan and parts of North Bengal and Assam one can still see the true richness of the jungle of the Himalayan foothills. Further south, in the Chittagong Hill Tracts of Bangladesh, there are large areas of unspoilt tropical wet evergreen forest in all its exuberance of impenetrable cane thickets, creeping bamboos, bromeliads and flowering epiphytes. Around clearings and along river banks immense hanging curtains of invasive Mikania vines and other creepers hang from the trees, their blossoms swarming with colourful Sunbirds, White-eyes and Flowerpeckers. The abundant fruits of the climbing figs are constantly consumed by various species of monkeys, green and pink pigeons and Hornbills. Exploring this region in 1966, I came across a tragic example of engineering miscalculation. At the Kaptai Dam, tens of thousands of hectares of ancient and magnificent forest had been needlessly drowned in 1960 because someone had mistaken the ultimate level to which the water would rise. Regiments of giant tree skeletons standing in the lake were all that remained of an area where once wild Elephants lived in the Karnaphuli wildlife reserve.

In the northern and eastern plains of India, at around the 1000 metre level, a very different type of much more open forest occurs – the Sal forest, where the beautiful Sal is the dominant species. Perhaps the most famous and still largely unspoilt tracts of Sal are in the Siwalik foothills and in the Kanha National Park in Madhya Pradesh. In the lower Indo-Gangetic plain the scene again changes – to patches of tropical dry deciduous forest rising to only about 23

The complex aerial roots of the _Banyan_ tree.

metres, with a light undergrowth of shrubs and grasses. Man's hand lies heavy on this region, and most of the trees are constantly lopped for firewood. Grazing cattle are everywhere, compounding the problem. Further south in the Deccan plateau and east of the Western Ghats there is thorn forest. The once extensive thorn forests of the Indus valley in Pakistan have long since been destroyed. Much of north-western India, where there is very little rainfall, is now either desert or has scattered patches of stunted Acacias and other drought-tolerant species. In the Thar Desert, a single plant species, _Prosopis juliflora_, provides almost the only fuel available to villagers and the only fodder for their cattle.

Finally, in the tidal creeks in the Sundarbans delta, the vegetation is again completely different, a closed evergreen tidal forest of some 20 species of mangrove trees, with an undergrowth of Pandanus Screw Palms, canes and other salt-tolerant shrubs.

The forests of north-east India, like those on the seaward side of the Western Ghats and in the Hill Tracts, are broadly classified as rain forests. Most visitors are deterred from exploring them because their margins alongside the occasional roads or rivers are usually walled in by a twisted mass of huge, sun-loving vines which are penetrable only by slashing a way through. The effort, however, is well worthwhile. Once beneath the high closed canopy, which is often 45-60 metres above ground, progress is relatively easy, little vegetation being able to grow in the gloom of the forest floor. The air is noticeably stagnant and humid and only occasional sparkles of sunlight can penetrate. The trees are of bewildering variety; as many as 100 different species have been identified within an area of one hectare. A single tree may be host to 500 different species of beetles. Some of the giant tree tunks, such as the Kapoks, have wide buttresses, others grow from a pyramid of stilt-roots. Here and there an immense strangling fig has wrapped its web of climbers around a big tree and killed it in the struggle to reach the sunlight far above. Other trees rise straight and magnificent, without branching until 30 metres above ground. Some of these giants have silvery-white bark, heightening the impression that you are walking in the nave of a dimly-lit cathedral. The litter on the forest floor teems with grotesquely formed insects and colourful fungi, all busily engaged in helping the myriads of unseen micro-organisms to break down the rotting leaves and fallen trees to provide the soil nutrients on which the forest lives. Decomposition is ten times more rapid than in a temperate forest. A tropical forest is never silent. By day there is the constant hum of flies, bees, wasps and hornets and by night the loud rasping chorus of countless cicadas and frogs.

There is little visible movement at ground level in a rain forest, except for the occasional passing of a sounder of Wild Pigs or a solitary Mouse Deer, but in the leaf canopy above there is a constant coming and going of monkeys, squirrels and birds, all feasting on the plentiful fruit, nectar or tender leaves. Stand still for a few moments and watch the ground, and you will see the ever-hungry leeches approaching from every quarter, looping their sinister way with uncanny skill towards the potential source of mammalian blood. A huge percentage of the billions of leeches which inhabit rain forests never succeed in getting a meal during their short lives. Any passing mammal is therefore an immediate victim. They drop in hundreds from the vegetation, alerted by the vibration of footsteps. It is almost impossible to escape their attention, and the speed with which they penetrate clothing and even the lace-holes in boots is astonishing. They are, however, easily removed with the aid of a lighted cigarette or a pinch of salt. If merely brushed off, they usually leave their suckers behind – the wound then bleeds for a long time because of the anti-coagulant which they exude, and it may become a tiresome sore. However, it is possible to get used to the leeches, and they are a small price to pay for seeing the many marvels of the rain forest.

There are many different kinds of rain forest in the equatorial regions of the world. All the various types are, alas, now disappearing before their scientific secrets or their potential values to man have been fully ascertained. At the present rate of destruction, which is estimated at more than 22 hectares per minute worldwide, there will be almost none left by the year 2020, apart from the sample areas of each type which many local governments, acting on the advice of the World Wildlife Fund (WWF) and the International Union for Conservation of Nature and Natural Resources (IUCN), are trying desperately to save for posterity.*

The Indian Government is well aware of the economic and social values of the declining vegetation of the country. In 1984 it launched a far-reaching programme of research and development for the protection of plant-life. This included the establishment of gene-sanctuaries for endangered species and biosphere reserves for representative areas of vegetation. Particular attention will be paid to preventing the over-exploitation of the medicinal plants on which 90 per cent of India's medicines depend. A supporting programme of education will be directed at schools, universities, botanic gardens, army establishments and village councils. The 1100 nature clubs created by the Indian branch of the WWF will play an active part in this.

The Riches of Wildlife

The wildlife of the Indian subcontinent, like its vegetation, emphasises by its diversity of species the widely differing habitats and climatic zones which are available. There are about 500 different mammals, more than 2000 species of birds and several hundred reptiles and amphibians. By comparison with Africa, however, the larger animals are more difficult to see, most of them living not out in open savanna as in Africa, but in forests; moreover, the majority are nocturnal, or at best crepuscular.

India was one of the very few countries whose Prime Minister for a number of decades had a very strong personal interest in the conservation of wildlife. Unfortunately, however, the late Mrs. Gandhi was unable to prevent the inexorable impact of Man on the natural environment. Nevertheless, the wise conservation policies which she introduced did much to reduce this impact. At the time of the British Raj, all the many books written by soldiers and government officials, most of whom were also hunters, gave the impression that game animals proliferated in such numbers as to seem inexhaustible. Certainly the great hunting parties organised by the Maharajahs in honour of local or visiting dignitaries suggested this by the quantities which they slaughtered year after year. One such

* The World Wildlife Fund (WWF), working in close partnership with its scientific advisers the International Union for Conservation of Nature and Natural Resources (IUCN), is the leading international charitable foundation concerned with the conservation of wildlife.

example was a *shikar* which in a few days in 1919 accounted for 120 Tigers, 27 Leopards and 18 Sloth Bears. Many Englishmen claimed to have shot 100 Tigers during their tours of duty in India. A few hunters claimed as many as 300, the record being held by the Maharajah of Surguja, who is on record as having declared that during his lifetime he had killed no fewer than 1150 of these animals. Many Maharajahs claimed their first Tiger at the tender age of twelve and continued shooting them until well into their seventies.

Tigers had been hunted even before the Indo-Aryans arrived in the Indus valley. The earlier Bronze Age Harappa civilisation used the image of a Tiger on its seals, and the first Moghuls are known to have enjoyed Tiger-hunting. It became the sport of kings and remained so for more than a thousand years. The dangerous pastime of hunting on foot with spears or bows and arrows gave the Tiger at least an even break. It was not until the invention of the matchlock gun in the 15th century that their odds began to shorten. By the 17th century, with the introduction of the flintlock and rifled barrel, they swung heavily against the Tiger and all other game animals. No animals stand a chance of survival against modern high-velocity rifles with telescopic sights. It was not hunting, however, which was the principal cause of the decline of wildlife in the subcontinent, but the progressive destruction of the forests where most of the animals lived.

Not until the late 1930s was the first voice raised in defence of the Tiger, when the great hunter-naturalist Jim Corbett published books expressing concern about their declining population. He prophesied, to the astonishment of many, that unless excessive hunting and the destruction of forests could be curbed, the Tiger would soon become extinct. Few believed him, because at that time it was thought that there were still at least 40,000 Tigers in India, to say nothing of those in the adjacent countries. This figure was, however, mere guesswork.

After the Partition of India and the turmoil which followed it, little thought was given to the subject. Law and order had broken down and villagers, who in the past had participated in hunting only as hired beaters, now had access not only to guns but also to the previously protected forests and hunting reserves. Tigers and other game animals were shot, trapped and poisoned everywhere and a thriving black market in skins was soon created. By the time law and order were re-established, it was several years before these practices could be brought under control. The process was not helped by the fact that, as soon as it was realised that Tigers were rapidly disappearing, hunters from all over the world hurried to India to bag one before it was too late. Tiger-skin rugs and coats were by then selling in New York, Paris and Tokyo for as much as $5000, and commercially sponsored hunting and smuggling became big business.

Meanwhile, the rapidly increasing human population, dizzy with the euphoria of Independence, was clamouring for land. The plains were already over-populated and the obvious solution was to exploit the previously protected forests, many of which had been owned by the now dispossessed Maharajahs. The speed with which forests disappeared in the following 30 years, not only in India but also throughout Asia, was accelerated by the world-wide demand for timber, which provided much-needed hard currency to the exporting countries. The effect on wildlife was devastating.

Tigers are essentially animals of the forest, as are their prey – the wild pigs and deer. Once deprived of their habitat they are doomed. The Indian Government, through the State Forest and Wildlife Departments, and encouraged by the Indian Board for Wild Life and the World Wildlife Fund, conducted a careful census in 1972 which revealed that only about 1826 Tigers survived in India. In Nepal, Sikkim, Bhutan, Bangladesh and western Burma, where the Indian race of the Tiger also occurs, there were perhaps a further 600-700. Throughout Asia, where the other seven races or subspecies occurred, a similarly catastrophic decline had been caused. The Caspian and Balinese races were already extinct. Only five Javan Tigers remained, only about 300 Siberian in the USSR and northern China and perhaps 500-1000 Sumatran. The Chinese race, by government edict, had been almost exterminated as 'harm-ful to agricultural and pastoral progress.' The Indo-Chinese, which had a huge range from eastern Burma to the China Sea, was thought to number about 2000. Thus a dominant animal species which in the 1930s had a probable total population in Asia of about 100,000, had dwindled in only 40 years to a mere 5000 or so. It was obvious that at such a rate of decline the Tiger would be totally extinct everywhere within a very few years.

The Tiger has always been my favourite animal, and I have studied its behaviour in the wild in four countries. It is also one of the world's most magnificent and best known animals. I therefore became closely involved in the international campaign which the World Wildlife Fund launched in 1971 to save it from extinction. The response was immediate and gratifying, nearly $2 million being subscribed by the public, world-wide. Thanks to the willing co-operation of a dozen countries in Asia, including the USSR and China (but not Burma), the Tiger was given legal protection and soon provided with more than 40 protected and well managed reserves. Under the Convention on the International Trade in Endangered Species, the export and import of Tiger skins was banned and their hunting was either banned or strictly controlled.

Operation Tiger, as the campaign was called, began in India, where the late Prime Minister, Mrs Indira Gandhi, set an example of government initiative which inspired the rest of Asia. Her interest in wildlife, inspired by her father Pandit Jawaharlal Nehru, was very real, and she made the Tiger the symbol of India's dedication to the preservation of all wildlife. In return for the promise of technical equipment and scientific assistance to the value of $1,000,000 from the World Wildlife Fund, the Indian Government launched its own Project Tiger, and has since created 15 Tiger reserves, on which it has spent ten times this sum. The money was used for the training, equipping and housing of guards, on building patrol roads, on improving water resources and fire control, on translocating vulnerable villages and on the management of the forests and grazing areas. Because the planning was on the basis of improving the entire ecosystem, not only the Tigers and their prey species benefitted, but also the whole spectrum of mammals, birds, reptiles, insects and vegetation. One of the important outcomes of skilled management has been that many previously seasonal streams in the reserves now flow perennially, to the benefit of the surrounding villages as well as the wildlife.

Signboard at the entrance to Bandipur Reserve.

The Tigers in the now strictly protected 25,000 square kilometres of the reserves are thriving and have more than doubled in number. Their value as a tourist attraction has been recognised. Now free from the menace of hunters, they are beginning to become accustomed to the sight of tourists on elephants and can even be seen in daylight in some reserves such as Kanha and Ranthambhor and the Royal Chitwan National Park in Nepal. The excellently equipped 'Tiger Tops' lodge in Chitwan, with its well trained guides and riding elephants, has become internationally famous, and tourists are also flocking to the Indian Tiger reserves.

Project Tiger had its opponents among the *shikar* organisers and outfitters, who saw their livelihood threatened; Tiger hunting used to be a lucrative business and wealthy Americans were prepared to pay as much as $20,000 for the privilege of killing a single animal. A more understandable opposition arose recently because of a sudden steep increase in the number of villagers killed by Tigers. The worst incidents were in the North Kheri region near the Dudhwa National Park, where in five years no fewer than 95 people are said to have been killed. Such an outbreak was obviously a very serious matter. Not unexpectedly, the *shikar* outfitters made capital of it and demanded a return to Tiger-hunting. However, Mr H. S. Panwar, Director of Project Tiger, refused to be panicked into taking precipitate action. Instead, he examined in detail the circumstances in which each attack had taken place. His conclusions were quite clear: in spite of every effort to prevent them, many hundreds of villagers had over-run the protective buffer zone around the Tiger reserve to a degree which put them at serious risk of daily confrontation. The savanna area between the protected forest and the agricultural region outside the reserve boundaries had been occupied and planted with sugar-cane right up to the forest edge. Sugar-cane is not unlike the tall grass and bamboo thickets in which Tigers habitually rest during the heat of the day, and they immediately adopted the plantations, thus bringing them very close to the populated area. Inevitably, villagers and Tigers met face to face in competition for the same ground. A significant sidelight in the investigation was that many of the villagers were killed either when stooping to cut grass or while defecating, thus presenting a much more animal-like and less frightening shape than an upright man, which Tigers normally avoid. Some of the Tigers were shot as man-eaters, though the investigation showed that not all of these had been guilty. The conclusion was obvious: the plan that all Tiger reserves should have protective buffer zones around them was correct and that if these are over-run, Tigers will react by defending their territories. The tragic lesson of North Kheri has been learned the hard way, and is unlikely to be repeated.

Tigers are not inherent man-killers and in normal circumstances go out of their way to avoid humans. I have never carried a gun when studying them, even on foot, except once when in an area of known man-eaters and even then had no cause to use it. In the ma-

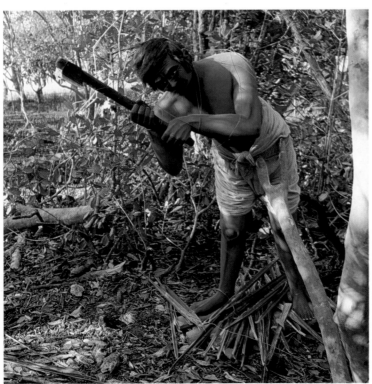

Sundarbans Tiger Reserve faces a problem with man-eating tigers which, over the years, have exacted a heavy toll from Bengali honey gatherers, wood-cutters and fishermen. To combat this situation, the Director of the reserve recently devised wooden effigies of human figures draped in *dhotis* and bearing a human scent. The figures are then wrapped with electrified wire and placed in selected positions in the mangrove forest. When a tiger attacks the figure, it receives a severe shock. Project Tiger staff are optimistic that this technique will soon prove an effective deterrent to tigers which attack humans.

jority of instances when they have been shot for attacking men it has been found that they did so because they were either starving, or were incapable of hunting their normal prey because of infirmity, shot-gun wounds or loss of teeth. In some parts of India tribal people have lived for centuries in forests where Tigers were numerous. Where there are still sufficient wild pigs and deer to satisfy the Tigers and where their habitat remains intact, outbreaks of man-killing very rarely occur. In fact, the tribal villagers are so casual about seeing them that they give them nicknames and make them keep their distance merely by shouting or beating tin cans. Neither side attempts to take over the territory of the other and they share the forest in a state of watchful harmony.

A small remnant population of Asiatic Lions still survives in the Gir National Park in the Indian State of Gujarat. They closely resemble the African Lion from which they originated, though the males usually have somewhat less heavy manes. I am an inclined to agree with the late E. P. Gee that this is probably not a natural evolutionary change but the result of selective hunting – the hunter always choosing the animal with the biggest mane. The range of the Asiatic Lion once extended from Greece through the Middle East to central India, but when I first visited the Gir in 1969 their world population stood at only 177 and was declining. The Gir forest had been the property of the local Moslem rulers, the Nawabs of Junagadh, who had protected the Lions since early in this century. When the last Nawab fled to Pakistan after the Partition of India, his land was speedily over-run by villagers and their cattle. Nearly all the deer had vanished and the Lions were obliged to feed on the thousands of domestic cattle, which were rapidly destroying the vegetation. Whenever Lions killed a cow, the *harijans* (the so-called 'untouchables,' who alone will dispose of dead animals) seized the carcass in order to sell the meat, bones and hide. The wretched Lions seldom got a square meal and were starving.

Dr Paul Joslin and I made independent studies of the Gir and I sent our recommendations to Mrs Gandhi. Thanks to her intervention and the efforts of the Gujarat State government, the Gir National Park was put under skilled management and has since become one of the best managed wildlife reserve in India. Nearly all the local graziers and some 20,000 cattle have successfully been resettled beyond its boundaries. With the recovery of the grazing areas, the population of various deer species has reached an astonishing level of 11,000 animals, and the Lions now have an abundance of their natural prey. By 1979, Leopards numbered 161 and Lions 205 (now 217) – but salvation came only just in time.

Unfortunately, the once abundant Cheetahs, of which some thousands of the Asiatic race used to be kept by the Indian Princes for hunting Chinkara Gazelles and Blackbuck, are now extinct in Asia, except for a very few in Iran and possibly one or two in the Mekhran coastal region of Baluchistan. The last apparently wild Cheetah in India was shot in 1947. The possibility of reintroducing the species by transfer from the small surviving Iranian population is now being considered, but I fear that the number available may be too small to justify the experiment.

The three leopard species, however, still survive, but only the common Leopard, which is a particularly adaptable creature, has maintained its original range. It now appears to live by preference near villages, where it preys on dogs, goats, calves and poultry. Usually called the Panther in India, it not infrequently occurs in an all-black form, through which the typical "rosette" markings 'are' still visible in sunlight. The so-called Black Panther is not, however, a true species but a morph, or colour phase, of the Leopard. Its relative, the beautiful Snow Leopard, is shot and trapped wherever it still occurs in the Himalayas, except in the Buddhist parts of Bhutan and Ladakh, for the value of its magnificent fur, which is creamy-white with large dark rosettes. Living above the snow-line, it preys on Marmots, Mountain Hares and the various mountain sheep and goats. In order to maintain a firm grip on ice it has evolved hairy soles to its feet. The largest surviving population is in the Jigme Dorji Reserve which H M King Jigme Singye Wangchuk of Bhutan created on the Himalayan border with Tibet. There are some Snow Leopards in Pakistan's high-altitude Khunjerab National Park, while the new reserves at Nanda Devi, Shey Dolpo and

Shey Phuksundo on the Tibetan border will also help to save this wonderful animal. Clouded Leopards, by contrast, are strictly arboreal tropical species, whose range is from southern Nepal eastward to China. Because of their short legs and very long canine teeth they have been likened to miniature Sabre-toothed Tigers, but these prehistoric beasts were not their ancestors. Their greyish-buff coats are heavily mottled with blackish blotches and they have abnormally long tails. With luck they can still be seen in northern Assam, Nepal, Bhutan and the Chittagong Hill Tracts.

Intermediate in size between the leopards and the smaller cats is the very attractive Golden Cat, which is well over a metre in length and with its unmarked tawny coat resembles a miniature Puma. It is said to occur in Assam, Nepal, Sikkim and the Hill Tracts eastward through Burma and Malaysia.

Of the six small cats, one, the strikingly long-haired Pallas's Cat of Tibet and Ladakh, is rarely seen, though skins appear occasionally in native markets. It has a distinctively flattened head and ears and hunts small rodents on high, rocky ground. Desert Cats and Jungle Cats are still fairly numerous in north-west to central India and in parts of Pakistan. Both have sandy coloration, the Jungle Cat being easily distinguished by its shorter, banded tail. The Desert Cat has hairy soles to its feet, enabling it to move swiftly in soft sand. The largest of the group is the Fishing Cat, which has a rough, greyish-tawny coat with rows of diffuse dark streaks and rather short legs. It is a fierce little animal which often takes dogs and poultry from fishing villages and has been known to attack children. It is found chiefly in reed-beds and jungle in the Indo-

A Jungle Cat in Ranthambhor Tiger Reserve.

Gangetic Plain, Orissa, the Malabar coast and the Indus delta in Pakistan. Like a domestic cat at a goldfish bowl it catches fish with a lightning-quick scoop of its semi-webbed paw. It swims strongly and, unlike other cats, also dives occasionally. Two other species, the pale buff, round-spotted Leopard Cat and the more heavily blotched Marbled Cat, which resembles a miniature Clouded Leopard in its markings, inhabit the Himalayan forests. A few of the former are also found in southern India, while the latter is chiefly restricted to the north-east. Both, although now legally protected, are heavily exploited by poachers for their beautifully marked skins. A recent study by the World Wildlife Fund and the Zoological Survey of India drew attention to the need to protect the habitats of all the small cats if they are to survive.

Two much larger felines are the Lynx and the Caracal. With their sandy coloration and upstanding tufted ears they are easily recognised. The former, which is a race of the European Lynx, is the larger of the two and is heavily built, with a very short, black-tipped tail. Occupying the highlands of Gilgit, Ladakh and Tibet up to an altitude of 3000 metres, it preys on birds, hares, rodents and occasionally wild sheep and goats. The more slender, longer-tailed Caracal inhabits the desert regions of Pakistan and India. It is a more agile hunter, sometimes killing even such fleet-footed creatures as Chinkara Gazelles. I once saw one stalk a flock of sandgrouse drinking at a water-hole, two of which it killed in a whirl-

wind attack. Caracals used to be trained to hunt bustards and peafowl, but have now become rather rare.

There are three species of bears in the Indian region, the Brown Bear, the Himalayan Black Bear and the Sloth Bear. All three are formidable animals which are frequently in conflict with man and are therefore often shot. The range of the Brown Bear is only just within the region, at high altitudes in the north-western and central Himalayas, being most numerous in Ladakh. In summer it descends below the treeline and, if food is scarce, plays havoc with domestic flocks, although its usual diet is fruit, roots and rodents. The Black Bear is still fairly numerous in the Himalayas, occasionally as high as the tree-line (3700 metres), but more often at lower altitudes. Occasionally a vagrant wanders as far south as Sylhet. Its footprints in the snow, with five clearly defined toes, are rather like those of a man, though the long claw-marks are easily distinguished. When the melting snow obliterates the claw-marks, the probable origin of the mythical Yeti remains for all to see. The Sherpas of Nepal are firm believers in the Yeti, but the remains of one exhibited in a Buddhist monastery have been proved to be an unconvincing fake.

Black Bears hibernate during the coldest part of the winter, in leaf-lined rock or earth caves. When they descend to the foothills in search of fruit they are frequently disturbed by woodcutters and farmers, whom they attack without hesitation if at close quarters. Dr Robert Fleming, a famous authority on Himalayan birds who at that time was a surgeon at the Kathmandu hospital, told me of scores of men brought to him with terrible wounds caused by the raking claws of Black Bears and that many had been hugged and bitten in the face.

The smaller Sloth Bear has much more shaggy and greyer fur than the Black, giving it a distinctly untidy appearance. It has a whitish 'V' on its chest, but this is less obvious than on the shining fur of the Black Bear. Its grey snout is disproportionately long, and when it is ambling along in its forest habitat it always strikes me as a rather ungainly caricature of its handsome relative. Feeding chiefly on fruit and insects, it also searches diligently for honey, climbing the highest branches for the hanging combs of wild bees, which, if it cannot reach them, it shakes down with great vigour. Sure signs that a Sloth Bear is about are the devastated termite mounds which it excavates and the huge pits which it digs in search of grubs. Orchards and plantations of sugar-cane are often raided, but humans are seldom attacked. One of the best places to see these animals is in the Royal Chitwan National Park in Nepal, when the new grass is just emerging and they are hunting in daylight for termite nests. Later, when the grass is high, they are more likely to be in dense forest, feeding on mangoes and wild figs. India now has two special reserves for Sloth Bears, at Dumkhal and Ratanmahal.

After the bears, it is inevitable to think next of the Red Panda, which also inhabits the Himalayan forests eastward across Asia. Pandas, however, are not bears, their closest relatives being probably the North American racoons. The present range of the Giant Panda of China does not extend to India, but its much smaller relation, the Red Panda, can be seen in the temperate forests of Nepal, Sikkim and Bhutan, usually in bamboo thickets above the 1500 metre level.

The Indian Elephant is a familiar sight as a domesticated animal throughout south-east Asia. It is slightly smaller than its African counterpart and easily distinguished by its smaller ears and rounded, rather than hollow, back. Its hind feet have four nails instead of the African's three and its trunk only a single 'lip'. The cows usually lack tusks and those of the bulls are seldom very large.

Being forest animals, they have suffered, like so many others, from the relentless erosion of their habitat. In the Indian subcontinent their largest surviving wild population is in the north-eastern forests, in North Bengal, Assam and Bhutan, where there are about 6500, plus perhaps another 200 in the Bangladesh Hill Tracts, between Tripura and the Burmese Arakan. In central India there are 2200 and in the north-west another 500, including those in Corbett. An isolated population of about 6000 exists in southern India at the junction of the three States of Karnataka, Kerala and Tamil Nadu.

Everywhere their numbers are declining.

Domesticated elephants are of great economic value, but their numbers are no longer sustained by recruitment from the wild. Elephant round-ups have now been suspended altogether and stocks are being supplemented from calves born from already domesticated cows. They are, however, difficult to breed in captivity, partly because it is almost impossible to control bulls when they are in *musth* and partly because cows with small calves cannot work for a long time. Calves do not begin work until 15 years old. The cows are therefore condemned to a life of celibacy and toil. Nevertheless they occasionally contrive to mate with wild bulls. On my last visit to Nepal my riding elephant suddenly gave birth to a delightful little bull calf, to the amazement of her *mahout*, who had been quite unaware that she was pregnant. She had evidently been mated one night while turned out to feed in the forest. The traditional method of recruitment, known as the *khedda*, involved driving wild elephants into stockades, where they were chained until trained. The rounding up and driving of wild herds caused great psychological disturbance to such sensitive creatures and this method was condemned by conservationists. It is no longer used today in India, though still practised in Bangladesh and Burma. The last *khedda* in India took place in the Nagarhole region in the 1970s. Another method formerly used in north-east India was the so-called *mela shikar*, in which wild elephants were lassooed from trained domestic elephants. Less harm and panic in the herd would arise if selected animals were dart-gunned with tranquilising drugs.

War elephants carved from stone in a 10th century wall frieze at the Lakshmana temple. Khajuraho.

A scientific symposium was held in 1982 at the Jaldapara wildlife reserve in North Bengal to examine the very difficult problem of the conservation and management of Indian Elephants. The problem is compounded by the obvious fact that the more wild populations are compressed by the growing destruction of their forest habitat, and the more groups become broken up and isolated, the greater the difficulty of controlling their ravages on plantations of oil-palm, sugar-cane, rice and other crops. When elephants are hungry it is extremely difficult to prevent them from doing serious damage. Crowds of villagers try to stop them by banging gongs, waving torches, throwing spears and shooting at them with crop-protection guns. The frightened elephants are then liable to charge the crowd and not only trample the crops, but sometimes also knock down village houses, killing people in the process. It was shown at the symposium that there are two practical means of preventing such losses. One is to station *koonkis* (domesticated elephants trained for the capture of wild ones) to guard the crops: wild elephants are apparently terrified by them, perhaps because of their close association with humans, although this does not prevent occasional mating with them when domesticated females are on heat. The other is to erect simple two-strand electrified fences, which the elephants soon learn to respect. Because of the difficulty of creating large enough special reserves, it is now proposed to establish 'Elephant Ranges', where the herds' requirements would be regarded

as paramount, but where compatible human activities would still be permitted. For example, selective logging and carefully controlled slash-and-burn cultivation can actually produce more food for elephants in the resulting secondary growth.

Plans are also now being considered for the creation of a protected elephant reserve of some 3500 square kilometres of forest extending from the Jaldapara reserve through northern Assam and including the Manas and Buxar tiger reserves which adjoin the frontier with Bhutan. The King of Bhutan has promised that the big Bhutan Manas reserve could be included, as well as some proposed new forest reserves. There is hope that a new national park shared by the three States where the southern Indian Elephants occur may represent a solution for the survival of a large part of that population. Both schemes await political sanction. In the Cox's Bazar Division of the Chittagong Hill Tracts a group of Bangladeshi scientists is studying the elephant survival problem in that region, hoping to create a protected reserve in the Taknaf Peninsula.

Riding a well-trained elephant is still incomparably the best method for seeing wildlife in India. I have often been able to approach Tigers and other big game animals to within ten or twelve metres by this means. Only a slowly paddled canoe on a river can compare with the silence of an elephant's progress through the jungle. Its instant response to a whispered command from the *mahout*, or to the pressure of his bare foot, is a revelation to those unaccustomed to the intelligence of these mighty animals.

In Nepal's Chitwan National Park, tourists are conveyed through the jungle for game viewing on trained elephants.

The second largest animal of the subcontinent is the Indian One-horned Rhinoceros. Of the world's five species, only the African White Rhinoceros exceeds it in weight. Its single stubby horn is rarely longer than 38 centimetres, the majority being much shorter. More than any other species it has a distinctly prehistoric appearance because of its massively folded hide, which is studded with rounded tubercules resembling rivet-heads, recalling the rivetted armour on a 1918 army tank. Formerly distributed throughout the Gangetic plain and even in the middle reaches of the Indus in Pakistan (where a pair from Nepal has recently been re-introduced in the Lal Suhanra reserve), it is now restricted to a very few areas, such as the Kaziranga National Park and Manas Reserve in Assam, the Jaldapara reserve in North Bengal and the Royal Chitwan National Park in Nepal. The total number surviving is about 1200 in India and 300 in Nepal and they are breeding successfully under protection. In order to widen the distribution, several rhinos were tranquilized in Assam in 1984 and transported to suitable habitat in the Dudhwa National Park in Uttar Pradesh.

Like the African and other Asian species, the One-horned Rhinoceros has suffered persistent persecution for the supposed medicinal, and to a lesser extent the aphrodisiac value, of its horn. In 1978 this was selling at $1500 per kilogram; by 1984 the price had risen to $8500. In recent years even higher prices have been paid in the Yemen Arab Republic, where ceremonial *jambiyya* daggers with rhino-horn handles are considered a status symbol, which many can now afford from their earnings as workers in the oil-rich Gulf States. Perhaps it is the extraordinary appearance and power of a rhino that have suggested magical properties to the superstitious, for every part of its carcass is valued. Even its urine is bottled and sold in Indian zoos as a cure for asthma. But to kill a 2½ ton rhino merely to cut off its horn, is like destroying a cathedral in order to steal the cross from its spire.

The much smaller Sumatran Rhinoceros, which once occupied the hills of Assam, still wanders occasionally from Burma into the Hill Tracts. In 1967 one was shot near Cox's Bazar and its carcass sold in small pieces in Chittagong for the equivalent of some $1200. The Javan Rhinoceros, which occurred in the Sundarbans until 1900, is nearing extinction in Java.

Indian Rhinoceroses are more solitary than their African relations. Like all rhinos they are rather morose and of uncertain temper, not hesitating, if accompanied by a calf, to charge an intruding elephant. In a close attack they slash upwards with their powerful incisors rather than with their horns. I have watched two bull rhinos fighting and the collision was like that of two high-speed trains. They can run surprisingly quickly and I have been more frightened by them at night when camping in their neighbourhood than ever I was by Tigers, which much prefer to avoid contact with humans. However, Indian Rhinoceroses can be observed without difficulty if one's elephant is well trained, as they are, for example, in the Kaziranga or Chitwan reserves.

Among the many even-toed ungulates of the subcontinent – the wild oxen, sheep, goats, deer, antelopes and pigs – the massive Gaur, or Jungle Bison, takes pride of place. Standing nearly two metres at the shoulder and weighing 900 kilograms or more, a bull Gaur is a magnificent animal. Its sleek hide is a gleaming black, with strikingly white 'stockings'. Its horns are short and curved and its enormous shoulders are ridged as far as the middle of its back. In spite of such an imposing appearance, however, Gaur are timid, forest-loving creatures, moving about in small family herds and descending from the hills to graze in the valleys at dawn and again in late afternoon. Their only enemy is the Tiger, which preys on the smaller cows and calves, very rarely tackling a full-grown bull. These splendid animals are now chiefly restricted to the eastern and southern hill forests. They can be seen in such wildlife reserves as the Bandipur in Karnataka State and the adjoining Mudumalai in Tamil Nadu. There are a few in the Kanha reserve in Madhya Pradesh and I have occasionally seen a herd in the western part of the Chitwan in Nepal when fresh grass was just emerging.

Gaur have never been domesticated, although hybrids with domestic cattle do occur occasionally. It seems possible that such crosses led to the creation of the Gayal, or Mithun, which resembles a rather small Gaur with straighter horns. Gayal are at least now and then domesticated, not as draught animals but for purposes of religious sacrifice, by some of the forest tribes such as the Moghs and Chakmas of the Hill Tracts. However, my companion Eric Hosking and I were once chased along a river bank in the Hill Tracts by a couple of bull Gayals, which gave no evidence whatever of being domesticated. Their charge was, in fact, rather spectacular.

Almost as massively-built as the Gaur, the Indian Wild Buffalo is a much more aggressive animal. Whereas domestic buffaloes are the epitome of docility and are led or ridden by tiny children in the paddyfields, their wild relatives are extremely shy of humans. They can be dangerous if approached too closely and not infrequently kill domestic bulls which show interest in their cows, Not many of them are left now and most of the survivors are restricted to the swampy grasslands and cane-brakes of Assam. The Kaziranga National Park and Manas Tiger Reserve are the best places to see them. They are also found in the Bastar forests of Madhya Pradesh and there used to be a few in the small Kosi Tappu reserve in Nepal, but I doubt that they will be able to stand up to the increasing exploitation of that area. Wild and domesticated Yaks can be seen

in the higher levels of Nepal and Ladakh and also Zums, which are hybrids between Yak cows and domestic Brahminy cattle.

The four species of wild sheep of the Himalayas can be seen only by those prepared to climb to the high altitudes where they live. They are all hunted by the hill tribes and, in spite of their being officially protected, are often also shot by foreign trophy hunters and embassy officials who bribe the local authorities. The most splendid of the four is the Marco Polo Sheep of the Hunza region and the Russian Pamirs, whose great outward-curving, deeply wrinkled horns are much more massive than those of the famous Big-horn Sheep of the American Rockies. The very similar Nayan, or Tibetan Sheep, of Ladakh, Nepal and Sikkim, have horns almost as large, although they never exceed a single circle, whereas those of the Marco Polo have an additional outward curve. Both are distinctive races, or subspecies, of the Argali Sheep of Tibet and Siberia. Much smaller and more numerous in the mountains of Gilgit, Astor and Ladakh are the various races of the smaller-horned Urial, or Shapu; other races occur in the Salt Range and Kirthar Range in Pakistan, where they are more easily seen. The rather curious Bharal, or so-called Blue Sheep, which occupies the Himalayas at altitudes of 3000 to 5000 metres in Ladakh, Nepal and Sikkim, is now regarded as more closely related to the goats. Its horns are smooth and curved backwards, giving it a somewhat typically goat-like character. It is extremely difficult to approach and because its slate-blue hide merges perfectly with the colour of the rocks, is very difficult to observe until it moves.

There are five species of wild goats, all living in the mountains and all amazingly agile creatures which appear to defy the laws of gravity with impunity. I have seen some of them, such as the Ibex, running at full speed down almost vertical rocks which offered no apparent footholds. Even the rather heavily-built and long-haired Markhor, which has massive corkscrew horns, leads his harem at astonishing speed when alarmed. The Wild Goat, or Sind Ibex, is very like the Ibex, but with a grey rather than a buffish coat; its long, curved horns are slightly shorter than the 1.40 metres attained by the Ibex. Both are found at the western end of the Himalayas, a smaller race of the Sind Ibex also inhabiting the southern Kirthar Range in Pakistan. Although shooting has reduced the populations of these species, the main reason for their decline has been the introduction of diseases, such as anthrax, carried by domestic goats. I have seen domestic flocks feeding at 4300 metres where Markhor and Urial were also present. The two other goat species, the Himalayan and the Nilgiri Tahrs, are very distinctive and have short, back-curved horns. The Himalayan lives among the most spectacular crags and sheer cliffs up to an altitude of 4500 metres and feeds on the lower forest slopes. It has a handsome golden-brown coat of long, shaggy hair. Its relative the Nilgiri Tahr, when adult, has a blackish-brown coat with a whitish patch on its lower back and lacks the heavy mane of the Himalayan species; it is found in the Nilgiri Hills and part of the Western Ghats up to an altitude of 1800 metres.

The subcontinent has three species of goat-antelopes, the Goral, the Serow and the Takin. All three have goat-like characteristics such as short, cylindrical horns and short tails, and live in the mountains. The rather sheep-like Goral also has some resemblance to a Chamois, except for its horns, which lack the latter's terminal hook. The Serow is much larger and more ungainly, with long, donkey-like ears and blackish-brown hide; a small number still occupy the Manipur Hills, the eastern forests of Mymensingh and the Hill Tracts. The Takin, which lives in the Bhutan Himalayas and the Mishmi Hills, is even more ungainly, with a heavy-lipped, cow-like face and dense, shaggy fur which brings to mind a Yak. Its thick neck and short curved horns, on the other hand, recall those of a Wildebeest, yet it has no obvious relatives except the North American Musk Ox, and is an altogether curious creature. Visitors to Bhutan can see Takin in the small reserve at Thimphu, the capital city.

The great herds of gazelles, antelopes and deer which once roamed the subcontinent have long since disappeared, although they could be seen in fair numbers until the 1940s. All of them, however, are still well represented in India's wildlife reserves. The dainty little Chinkara Gazelle is the most agile of the group and, although exterminated in most of its former range, still survives in the Indian deserts and the open plains of the Deccan, as well as in the foothills of the Salt Range and in some other semi-desert areas of Pakistan. The little-known Tibetan Gazelle and the long-horned Tibetan Antelope occur in the northern parts of Ladakh. The handsome Blackbuck, the only true antelope of the region, was the favourite target of hunters from the days of the Moghuls onwards and was very nearly exterminated. Fortunately, many Maharajahs kept captive herds in order to enjoy the sport of seeing them chased and killed by captive Cheetahs or packs of dogs and some of these herds have survived. There is now a special Blackbuck sanctuary in the Velavadar National Park in Gujarat and at Talchappar in Rajasthan. In Pakistan they had almost totally disappeared by the 1960s, but with the aid of the World Wildlife Fund some were re-introduced into the Lal Suhanra reserve in Cholistan from, of all places, Texas, where huge herds originally introduced from India are now thriving in thousands on some of the big ranches. Others have since been introduced to Pakistan from India. Such co-operation in spite of political differences is very gratifying to conservationists.

The Four-horned Antelope is a solitary little animal which inhabits the tall-grass hilly regions of India. It is the only species with two pairs of short, spiky horns, which are carried by the male only. Standing barely 60 centimetres high, it is difficult to observe, but its shrill, whistling call can frequently be heard.

Few animals are more ungainly than the Nilgai, whose name means 'blue cow'. Although related to the elegant antelope family, everything about it looks wrong. Its horns look uselessly small (though surprisingly, one recently killed a man in Bhopal); it is too high at the shoulder and too sloping at the haunches; when it gallops, it does so in an ungainly giraffe-like manner and holds its head unnaturally high. Yet it is a successful animal, perhaps chiefly because its cow-like appearance prompts Hindus to give it religious protection and Moslem hunters to disdain shooting such a worthless creature.

Of the nine deer species, the most familiar is the Chital, or Spotted Deer, which, with its closely spotted rufous coat, is often regarded as the most beautiful of the world's many deer. For this reason it is a favourite in parks and zoos. In the wild it can be seen in most of the forests below the Indian Himalayas.

The four largest deer are the Sambar, the Barasingha, the Thamin and the Hangul. The last-mentioned, which is also called the Kashmir Stag, is the most seriously endangered. Closely resembling the European Red Deer, these handsome animals are restricted to the moist temperate forests in the northern part of Kashmir. They are most easily seen in the Dachigam Wildlife Sanctuary, a few miles north of Srinagar and perhaps in the Gamul Siya-Behl reserve in Himachal Pradesh. The Sambar, India's largest deer, is by contrast still doing fairly well. The heavily-maned stags carry long, powerful antlers which divide into two forks, with long, curved brow-tines.

The Barasingha, or Swamp Deer, is paler in colour than the Sambar. Its antlers are readily distinguishable because they branch into numerous, up-turned points and the brow-tines are more curved. Three distinct races are now recognised: *Cervus d. duvauceli* which has slightly splayed hooves and lives in swampy areas of the Nepalese terai; *C.d. ranjitsinhi* in similar habitat in Assam, and *C.d. branderi* with smaller, closer hooves appropriate to the hard, open ground where it lives in Madhya Pradesh. The largest concentrations of the *duvauceli* race are along the Nepalese frontier, where a particularly fine herd of 2600 can be seen in the Dudhwa National Park created by my old friend Billy Arjan Singh. There is another large population in the Sukla Phanta reserve in western Nepal, which I helped to create in 1972. The Kaziranga National Park in Assam is the main region of the *ranjitsinhi* race. The *branderi* race is easily seen in the Kanha reserve in Madhya Pradesh, which in my opinion, is the best in India.

In the low scrub-jungle of south-east Asia lives the Thamin, or Brow-antlered Deer. Its range extends westward only as far as the Manipur region of India, where it can still be seen in the *phumdi*, the floating swamp of Keibul Lamjao National Park. It resembles the Barasingha except for its distinctively curved antlers, forming a forward-pointing semi-circle from the brow-tine to the tip, which has only three or four rather blunt points.

There are four much smaller deer species: the Muntjac, the Hog Deer, the Musk Deer and the tiny Chevrotain, or Mouse Deer. The first two are quite numerous. Muntjac, or Barking Deer, stand 75 centimetres at the shoulder and have stubby little 7 centimetre antlers with two prongs, which rise from distinctive pedicles near the eyes. They live in thickly wooded hills along the Himalayas and in the central and southern Indian forests. Though shy, their dog-like barking call is easily imitated and I once called one out to the edge of a forest track by this means.

The origin of the Hog Deer's name is obvious: its rotund shape and pig-like movements as it scuttles through the undergrowth; with its head held very low. Although related to the well-antlered Chital, the Hog Deer male has very small two-pointed antlers like the Muntjac, but also two little brow-tines. Its habitat is dense grass along river-banks and in the plains, where it suffers heavy predation by Leopards and other large cats. Even Tigers do not disdain such tasty little creatures, pouncing on them in the long grass as a domestic cat will on a field mouse.

Musk Deer have been seen at 8000 metres in the Himalayas, but they live mainly in the high birch forests above the conifers in the mountains from Ladakh and Kashmir through Nepal to Bhutan. Two other races live in Siberia and southern China, where they are farmed. They are distinctive little animals, with very round bodies, elongated heads and large ears, but no antlers. Their so-called musk-pods, which lie beneath the abdominal skin of the male, have been their downfall, being highly prized as a base for the manufacture of perfumes and for various medicinal purposes throughout Asia, although medical research denies that they have either physiological or therapeutic value.

Finally, there is the elusive little Chevrotain, or Mouse Deer, a delightful Walt Disneyesque animal not much larger than a rabbit. It has delicate, pencil-thin legs, with four toes to each foot and a striped and spotted body. Like the Musk Deer, it lacks antlers and has projecting canine teeth. It is difficult to believe that these miniature creatures, flitting like small shadows through the litter on a forest floor, are deer, though of primitive form. It seems astonishing that they survive the constant predation of the many carnivores, birds of prey, Eagle Owls and Pythons which share the forest with them.

Only one species of the horse family is found in the subcontinent – the Wild Ass. There are two races, the Indian, which is now restricted to Gujarat, and the Tibetan, which occurs in the Ladakh area of Jammu and Kashmir. Herds of the Indian race used to roam in thousands across the desert regions of India and Baluchistan, but today it can be found only in the saline clay desert of the Little Rann of Kutch, which it shares with Chinkara Gazelles and Nilgai. A few occasionally wander into the Great Rann on the frontier between Gujarat and the Thar Desert in Pakistan. Living in a frontier region, they have been much persecuted by soldiers, who enjoy chasing them in jeeps. In Pakistan the soldiers assured me they never shot Wild Asses, but that local poachers did so in order to make suitcases out of their tanned hides. An adjacent military firing range is another hazard. It seems likely, however, that the decline in the population of Asses is mainly the result of competition for the very limited grazing by domestic cattle and of diseases such as African horse fever which the latter have introduced. Their population, which stood at about 5000 in 1960, has now dropped to below 2000. The Little Rann has been declared a Wildlife Reserve, but the future for the Indian Wild Ass remains a cause for concern. Other races of the species still survive in Tibet, Mongolia and Iran. The Syrian race is now extinct.

The dog family is well represented. Wolves have become scarce in India, where only 500-800 remain; but they can still be seen in the barren highlands of Kashmir and Ladakh and in the desert regions of India and Pakistan, where they take a toll of domestic cattle, goats and sheep. In Ladakh, Wolves are trapped in deep stone pits baited with a tethered donkey, but elsewhere they are usually poisoned, or shot while attacking domestic flocks. Those living on the Tibetan plateau are almost black and have much longer fur than the lowland Wolves of Pakistan and peninsular India. Occasionally, when hungry, they take to killing children around villages, although nowadays reports of such behaviour have diminished. Striped Hyenas and Jackals are fairly common everywhere and are useful scavengers, the former nevertheless being much disliked for their habit of disinterring human corpses. The weird and ghostly crying of jackals at night used to be one of the typical sounds of India. In chorus it has a nightmare quality though less frequently heard today. Foxes, too, are numerous and there are three distinctive races of the Eurasian Red Fox – the Hill Fox, the Desert Fox and the White-footed Fox. Another species, the Indian Fox, occurs in southern India.

Probably the most interesting canine is the Dhole, or Wild Dog. Like its African counterpart it is gregarious, hunting in packs, all members of the group helping to feed the young. Larger than the Jackal, it has a rufous colour and inhabits the forested regions from the Himalayas to the peninsula. It hunts in daylight, the pack pursuing its quarry at a relentless, loping gait, accelerating with a chorus of excited yapping in the final climax when the victim is surrounded and brought down. I find this sound particularly thrilling and full of menace. The communal skill of a hunting pack is impressive. A herd of deer is first stampeded, then a sickly animal or a fawn is cut out and separated from the herd and the chase begins. The victim very seldom escapes. If deer are scarce, Dhole packs do not hesitate to take on such formidable animals as Gaur, Buffalo, young Rhinoceroses or even Tigers, although many members of the pack may be killed in such encounters.

Monkeys are part of almost every Indian scene, crowding around villages and boldly entering cities, where they help themselves to food at wayside stalls and mingle with the traffic. They are rarely molested, although a few species such as the Golden Langur of the Sankosh River region on the Bhutan frontier are killed for their beautiful fur.

The commonest monkey in northern India is the Rhesus Macaque, which is distinguished from all other species by its red bottom. It can be seen around every town, temple and railway station, begging for food. There are five related and more localised species – the slightly larger Assamese Macaque, which does not have the characteristic red bottom, the Stump-tailed Macaque of the Himalayan foothills, the Pig-tailed Macaque of the Naga Hills, with an up-standing arched tail, the long-tailed Bonnet Macaque of the southern peninsula and the handsome but scarce Lion-tailed Macaque of the Malabar rain forests in the Ashambu Hills of the Western Ghats, the Anaimalai Sanctuary in Tamil Nadu and the Nell-

campathi Hills in Kerala. The Lion-tailed has a luxuriant mane of whitish hair and a tufted tail; destruction of its habitat has reduced its population to barely 800 and it is now listed as an endangered species which is carefully protected.

The second most plentiful monkey is the Common Langur, also known as the Hanuman Monkey. Shrines to the monkey-god Hanuman are numerous, particularly in Nepal. All the Langur species are extremely agile, long-limbed and long-tailed; their tails are not, however, prehensile like those of the South American monkeys. Common Langurs inhabit most Indian forests and I have seen them both at sea level and at 3500 metres in the Himalayas, where they have a particular fondness for eating rhododendron flowers. It is a delight to watch them leaping from tree to tree along the highways, or posed in graceful groups on the steps of ancient temples. They are invaluable companions in the jungle, giving immediate warning of the presence of Tigers or Leopards, which they follow with excited chattering from the safety of the tree-tops. The beautiful Golden Langur has already been mentioned. In addition there is the capped Langur of Assam and the Chittagong Hill Tracts and the Southern, or Nilgiri, Langur of the Western Ghats. Occasionally the closely related Phayre's Leaf Monkey occurs in Tripura and Bangladesh. My expedition of 1967 discovered and filmed in Sylhet a previously unrecorded species which proved to be a small colony of Dusky Leaf Monkeys; these were evidently vagrants from Burma.

The Hoolock Gibbon is the only true ape in the subcontinent, where its range extends from Burma into the forests of Assam and the Bangladesh Hill Tracts.

Two very small but fascinating little primates also inhabit the region – the Slow Loris and the Slender Loris. Although strictly nocturnal and very secretive, and therefore unlikely to be seen, they are often kept as pets in forest villages, where visitors may come across them. They belong to the Lemur family and have enormous, owl-like eyes and very round, pale, furry bodies. Feeding at night in the trees, they move in ultra-slow motion until they come upon an insect, which is then grabbed with both hands. Their grip is vice-like and quite difficult to release. The Slow Loris is the larger of the two, with a length of about 30 centimetres. The Slender Loris is barely 23 centimetres long and has prominent ears and grotesquely spindly little legs. It is a rather pathetic sight to see these inoffensive small creatures with such big-eyed, infantile expressions, tied to a post in full sunlight, for they need the darkness of dense forest and will not survive for long on village tit-bits.

Villagers in India also frequently keep captive civets and mongooses, both of which are easily tamed. There are half a dozen civet species, the most common being the Large and the Small Indian Civets, which are readily recognised by their boldly banded tails. All have long, sinuous bodies and long tails, with rather short legs and pointed muzzles. The Small Civet is seen everywhere except in high forest, whereas the Large is chiefly restricted to the Himalayan region. Both are omnivorous, with an unfortunate liking for raiding chicken coops and orchards. Another widespread species is the Palm Civet, or Toddy Cat, which is also frequently domesticated and can be seen scavenging in towns as well as villages. Unlike the two previously mentioned, it has a plain, unbanded tail. All the civets are useful as voracious and skilled hunters of rats.

For sheer agility and non-stop activity, no animals surpass the mongooses, of which there are five species in India and Pakistan. The one most widely seen both in the wild and as a domestic pet is the common Grey Mongoose. Many Europeans have learned to their cost that while mongooses make enchanting and affectionate pets, the speed with which they can totally wreck the curtains, cushions and ornaments in a home has to be seen to be believed. These world-famous little animals, immortalised by Rudyard Kipling's *Rikitikitavi*, invariably draw crowds when exhibited by snake-charmers in contests with cobras. The fact that the snakes have usually had their poison-glands drained or removed makes little difference, because the mongoose's erected bristling fur and lightning reactions protect it. Nevertheless, in the wild, mongooses, though remarkably resistant to snake poison, do occasionally succumb to the bite of a Cobra or a Krait. Villagers keep them

The Lion-Tailed Macaque is a localised species from the *shola* forests of the Western *Ghats* in south-western India. Today it is under severe threat of extinction due to habitat destruction.

as pets not only to combat snakes, but to control rats, mice and scorpions, which are obviously relished.

The Small Indian Mongoose, which is only half the size of the Grey, is also widespread and hunts in daylight. A distinctive race called the Desert Mongoose has a pale sandy colour, but is almost rufous in the Sind desert, where family parties hunt mice and gerbils. There are three larger, much less common species, the Stripe-necked of the Western Ghats, the Brown of southern India and the interesting Crab-eating Mongoose of Nepal and Assam. The last-mentioned species is the only aquatic member of the family, swimming and diving like an otter and feeding on fish, crabs and frogs.

In the Himalayan and southern parts of India, local races of the European Otter are found, while the very similar Smooth Otter occupies the whole region except for desert areas. One of its strongholds is the Sundarbans, where it is trained to drive fish into nets. Nets are lowered between two boats and the otters skilfully circle and drive the fish into them. Afterwards they climb on board, where each is given a fish, which is munched with little chirruping cries of obvious satisfaction. The otters are then permitted a siesta and a grooming session before renewing their work. The Bengali fishermen seem fond of their willing helpers and treat them well. The smaller, so-called Clawless Otter (which nevertheless has rudimentary claws) is very locally distributed only in some hill regions, the plains of Assam and lower Bengal.

Apart from the three otters, the fauna of the subcontinent is enriched by nearly two dozen other species of the family Mustelidae – the various martens, weasels, polecats, ferret-badgers, badgers and ratels. Then there are the Insectivores – the various shrews, hedgehogs and moles. And the very numerous families of bats and rodents, squirrels and flying squirrels, the porcupines and the hares, the pigs and the pangolins.

A familiar animal of the temperate Himalayan and Assamese forests is the handsome Yellow-throated Marten, which occurs at altitudes below 3000 metres. It is an agile hunter high in the trees or on the ground, occasionally killing animals as large as young Musk Deer, but usually preying on squirrels and birds, including pheasants and Snow Partridges. It has a fondness for fruit and the nectar of the Silk Cotton tree flowers, which it helps to pollinate. Its distinctive southern relative, the Nilgiri Marten, has more uniformly dark brown upper-parts and reddish forequarters. On the upper forest edges the Indian race of the European Stone Marten is fairly common as far east as Sikkim. Between 2400 and 4500 metres is the habitat of the Long-tailed Marmot and above them live the shorter-tailed Himalayan Marmots. Both are colonial-breeding and are familiar to all trekkers at these heights, sitting at the entrances of their burrows. I find their shrill whistling alarm cries rather welcome and reassuring in the oppressive silence of the high barrens.

Choosing from a long list of Indian bats, the great Fox Bat, or Flying Fox, can scarcely be missed as it is so conspicuous in many towns in India, Pakistan and Bangladesh. Its electrocuted corpses hang from countless power lines, looking like broken umbrellas. At dusk great flocks sally forth to feed on mangoes, figs and bananas. By day the flocks hang upside-down like giant fruits from the trees in city parks, cackling noisily and fanning themselves with their black wings. They are handsome creatures, with bright rufous fur and dog-like heads. In flight their wings have a spread of more than one metre and are flapped slowly, giving a crow-like rather than a bat-like impression. Like their smaller relatives the Fruit Bats, they are useful as pollinators of the fruit-bearing jungle trees, carrying pollen on their heads from tree to tree when feeding or drinking nectar from the flowers. The very striking Painted Bat also deserves mention; with brilliant orange, vermilion and black patterned wings it has been described as the most colourful mammal in the world. It is, however, a solitary species and seen only by good fortune.

A considerable number of very beautifully coloured squirrels and flying squirrels inhabit the forests. A few, such as the Kashmir Woolly Flying Squirrel, live at high altitudes in the Himalayas and have very copious fur to withstand the cold. Although some are as large as rabbits, they glide from tree to tree for quite astonishing distances on the extended membranes between their wrists and ankles, looking like flying tea-trays. Among the small squirrels, the species which every visitor to the subcontinent will see is the little Palm Squirrel, which in northern India and Pakistan usually has five stripes along its back and in the south three. It must be one of the most numerous and widespread of all the local animals. With its striped back and self-confident behaviour it is invariably likened by visiting Americans to the rather similar American Chipmunk.

Driving at night in forested regions, motorists often see Indian Porcupines crossing the road; the great mounds of earth which they excavate at the entrances to their burrows are conspicuous in many areas. These powerful animals, which can weigh as much as 18 kilograms, do a lot of damage to rootcrops and also de-bark fruit trees. They can be kept in captivity only in concrete enclosures, or they will dig their way to freedom in a matter of minutes. In the wild they are almost invulnerable to predation because of their long, bristling quills. Leopards appear to be the only predators which occasionally succeed in killing them, which they do by going for the unprotected head. Tigers, which are less agile, cannot resist trying to kill them, but invariably the Porcupine backs swiftly into its pursuer, driving its quills into the Tiger's face and chest. Dead Tigers have been found with festering quills embedded even in their lungs.

Another conspicuous animal, which is often seen tethered to a post in a village, is the armour-plated Indian Pangolin. Also called the Scaly Anteater, its body and tail are protected by strong, overlapping scales. When frightened, it instantly curls up into a tight ball. I once tried to pry open this defence but found the muscular contraction impregnable. The Pangolin is an inoffensive animal, which feeds on termites and ants and has a dignified, ambling gait, walking with the long, curved claws of its fore-feet turned inwards to support its weight. It is still fairly plentiful in the lowland areas and is replaced in Nepal by the smaller Chinese Pangolin.

The rare and elusive Pygmy Hog of northern Assam.

Wild Pigs represent a considerable economic problem because of their devastation of crops. In areas where the Tigers and Leopards which control their numbers have been exterminated, the farmers now recognize the value of these predators and are suffering heavy losses. A full-grown boar is a formidable animal. It can weigh more than 200 kilograms and is capable of killing even a Tiger with its powerful 20-centimetre tusks. A tiny and defenceless relative, the Pygmy Hog, was believed to be extinct by 1958, but was rediscovered in 1971 on the Paneery tea estate in Assam. I had the pleasure of handling a female in captivity. It measured only 26 centimetres at the shoulder, had no tusks and only three pairs of teats instead of the six of the Wild Pig. A small population of these delightful little animals is now carefully guarded in the Manas Reserve.

Finally, two interesting and related aquatic mammals deserve mention, the Gangetic and Indus Dolphins. Five species of dolphins and the Little Indian Porpoise can be seen in the estuaries or off-shore waters of the subcontinent. The Gangetic and Indus Dolphins have been the subject of long research and are now listed as endangered species. Unlike most of their kind they are not gregarious. They have only rudimentary eyes and feed on crustaceans on river-beds, rarely if ever entering salt water, although descending into semi-saline estuaries where they are frequently caught in fish-nets. They occur far inland in the Ganges, Brahmaputra and Indus.

I have seen Gangetic Dolphins as far inland as the Rapti River in Nepal. A study is being made of the survival problems of the Indus species and the government has established a sanctuary area for them between the Sukkur and Guddu barrages, where they are beginning to increase in number under protection.

A Paradise for Birds

The Indian subcontinent is a positive paradise for both amateur bird-watchers and serious ornithologists. If Sri Lanka is included, it has 2061 species and distinctive subspecies of birds, a figure surpassed only in South America. Europe has a mere 630 or so, including vagrants. As my friend Peter Jackson has shown, it is possible to see 150 different species in a single day on a car journey around the Delhi area including Sultanpur, where a reserve has been established. On my various explorations I have managed to see only about 800, or considerably less than half of the total species. The reason for this is that many of them are restricted to very small and remote areas. The great diversity of species is, of course, again a reflection of the many different climatic and vegetational zones available for their development.

Although the majority of birds are of tropical Oriental origin, an almost equal number originated either in the African or the Palaearctic (that is to say European or north Asian) regions. About 300 species, chiefly ducks, cranes, shore-birds, swallows and flycatchers, are migrants which enter India from central Asia at each end of the Himalayas, either down the Indus valley, or from northeastern Asia by way of the Brahmaputra. Some of the birds pass directly over the Himalayas. Bar-headed Geese, for example, have been seen over the peak of Everest itself, in other words flying at an altitude of about nine kilometres above sea level! The Rajah of Punial gave me an identification ring taken from the leg of a migrant Bar-headed Goose which he had shot crossing the high peaks of Hunza; later investigation showed that it had been ringed in north-central USSR. Many other species are merely altitudinal migrants, passing regularly back and forth from the high mountain slopes only as far as the valleys to breed. But a few, such as the hardy Snow Partridge and Snow Pigeon, contrive to nest successfully at an altitude of 5000 metres. For ornithologists interested in mass migration there are two much favoured Himalayan areas. One is the Kali Gandaki gorge, between the 8000 metre peaks of Annapurna and Dhaulagiri; the other is the high valleys of Ladakh, which are more difficult of access for the average visitor.

Birds are seldom molested in India. There is however a thriving export trade of about 2,000,000 wild-caught birds every year, chiefly the small, colourful finches, parakeets and mynahs, for the foreign cage-bird market. An extremely high mortality is involved, 50 percent or more of the birds being dead on arrival. A total of 300 species are involved in this nefarious trade.

Among the most extravagantly colourful birds are the numerous parakeets, woodpeckers and kingfishers, which are easily observed. Noisy flocks of the emerald-green Rose-ringed and Large Parakeets are common in many cities, the former nesting confidently beneath roof-tiles or in holes in wayside trees. Unfortunately, though so beautiful, their flocks do serious damage to grain crops. I have seen as many as 250 on a single field of millet. They are successful and invasive birds. Not long ago someone thoughtlessly released some Rose-ringed Parakeets in southern England and already they are multiplying and competing for nest-holes with local British birds. Their smaller relative the Blossom-headed Parakeet occupies the forested areas from Nepal southward and the Murree Hills in Pakistan. In the moist deciduous forests of the lower Himalayan region one finds the Red-breasted Parakeet and at higher altitudes, the whole length of the mountain range, the Slatey-headed Parakeet. The short-tailed green and crimson Lorikeet is more restricted to the eastern hills, Bangladesh and the Bombay region.

There are no fewer than 28 different kingfishers. They vary in size from the big Stork-billed, which is as large as a Jackdaw, to the tiny, jewel-like Three-toed, little bigger than a European Wren.

Nearly all are brilliantly coloured. Some, such as the Black and White Pied and Lesser Pied, frequent almost every stream, pond and water-tank, others are found only in tidal and coastal regions. Some are fish-eaters, others occur far inland in dry areas and feed on locusts, lizards, mice and small birds. The russet-coated Ruddy Kingfisher favours open secondary jungle and tea plantations; it has the intriguing habit of nesting in the globular communal nests of ferocious tree-ants without evicting them. The ants merely seal-off their passage-ways to the bird's nest cavity. A South American woodpecker, the Campo Flicker, has a rather similar habit of nesting in occupied termite mounds. In particularly rich feeding areas, such as the mangrove swamps of the Sundarbans, many kingfisher species occupy the same habitat, though selecting different food and therefore without competing.

Two other very colourful and numerous families are the sunbirds and the bee-eaters. Many Western visitors to India take the sunbirds to be hummingbirds because of their darting flight, iridescent plumage and habit of taking nectar from flowers. Hummingbirds, however, are restricted to the Americas. The 25 species and subspecies of Indian sunbirds not only have longer legs, but also normal wings instead of the stiff, narrow wings of the typical hummingbird. Their more soberly coloured relatives, the Spider-hunters, are readily distinguished by their very long, decurved bills. The ten different bee-eaters have a graceful swallow-like flight and colourful plumage, although perhaps none quite compares with the spectacular Carmine Bee-eater of Africa. Another brilliantly coloured bird which few visitors to India or Pakistan are likely to miss seeing perched on wayside telephone posts is the Indian Roller. In flight it displays a striking combination of shining light blue, dark blue and orange. About the size of a Jay, it gets its name from its aerobatic tumbling display-flight.

Although the subcontinent lacks the great variety of truly melodious song-birds found in Europe and North America, it has several which compare very favourably. Probably the best of these is the Shama, a beautiful but rather shy blue-black and chestnut bird with a long tail. To my mind its song equals that of a Nightingale for purity and of an American Mockingbird for variety. Not surprisingly, some Indian girls are named Shama. Its cousin the black and white Magpie-Robin can be seen in every garden.

The hornbills are another spectacular family of birds which inhabit the mature forests of India, Nepal, Bhutan and Bangladesh. All have grotesquely large bills and share the habit of walling-up their females in their nest-holes until the young are nearly fledged. This strange practice provides maximum security against predators and particularly from snakes. The sitting bird easily defends the small aperture through which she and the nestlings are fed by the male. There are five species, the largest being the Great Indian Hornbill, which is more than a metre in length, with boldly marked black and white wings and tail. In flight, its very broad wings make a distinctive singing note, like that made by those of a Mute Swan. This fine bird used to be quite numerous in the high forests of the Western Ghats, Assam and the Chittagong Hill Tracts; but all the hornbills are now suffering from the loss of the big trees on which they depend for nest-holes and also from the fact that their flesh and fat are believed by many forest tribes to have medicinal value. During the Burma campaign, when fresh meat was very scarce, I once ate a hornbill which had been shot by a Naga tribesman with a bow and arrow. I recall that it tasted somewhat rank, doubtless because hornbills eat lizards and snakes, as well as fruit.

Hindus regard Peafowl as sacred. Semi-tame flocks can be seen in many city parks and reserves, where they are decorative rather than interesting. I prefer to see them wild and in their full magnificence, when at dawn they come flying down the steep forested slopes of the Himalayan foothills, with the great trains of the males trailing behind them. The colourful Junglefowl, ancestors of all our domestic chicken, are also best seen and heard at dawn, when the cocks challenge the rising sun with a ringing 'cock-adoodle-doo'.

Birds of prey are relatively little persecuted by comparison with Europe and can be seen everywhere. Black Kites scavenge for refuse in every town and village and nest on roofs and window-sills. The handsome chestnut and white Brahminy Kites are almost equally numerous over sea-ports and fishing villages. Four common species of vultures, the White-backed, the Long-billed, the crimson headed King and the much smaller, yellow-faced Egyptian, swarm over the numerous carcasses of dead animals and also over the 'towers of silence' where Parsees leave their dead to be devoured. The long-winged Lammergeyer, or Bearded Vulture, like the Himalayan Griffon Vulture, is chiefly restricted to the Himalayas. There are about 20 species of large and small eagles, of which the rather lethargic Tawny is the most common, also half a dozen falcons and a similar number of hawks and harriers. In Pakistan the Peregrine and its close relatives the Saker and Lanner Falcons are in constant demand by Arab falconers, who pay very high prices for them. In Sind and Punjab they are caught by desert tribesmen during their migration. A man hides in a pit over which a trellis of branches is placed. A pigeon or a dove is tethered to the branches and made to flutter until it catches the eye of a passing falcon. When the falcon stoops on the decoy, the man in the pit seizes it by the legs. Many of these birds reach Europe and the Middle East illegally and are eagerly bought for $2000 or more, in spite of the heavy fines now imposed in some countries for possessing wild-caught falcons.

The bustard family, like the falcons, also suffers serious persecution and again it is the oil-rich Arabs from the Middle East who are the principal culprits. The species chiefly concerned is the Houbara Bustard. These handsome, turkey-like birds migrate each winter from the Aral Sea region in the USSR where they breed, to the deserts of Pakistan, Baluchistan and India, where they feed on the plentiful locusts. Every year hundreds of sheikhs and their numerous retinues arrive in Pakistan with fleets of Land-Rovers fitted with balloon sand-tyres in order to fly their falcons at Houbaras. Some years they kill as many as 3000. No scarce birds can withstand such a slaughter, and Russian conservationists have complained of a 75 per cent decline in the breeding population since the hunting in Pakistan began. Having exterminated the Houbara in their own countries, the Arabs have now agreed to support a research and breeding project and the Pakistan government, in spite of benefiting financially from the annual invasion of rich falconers, has introduced restrictions on the number of birds which may be taken. A total ban would be well merited.

Stone plaques at Bharatpur record wildfowl shoots of former days.

The larger and much more rare Great Indian Bustards live in even more parlous a situation. Standing one metre high and with long legs, they resemble miniature ostriches. Unfortunately they also represent to hungry people nearly 5 kilograms of meat and their population has been reduced to a dangerously low level of only 750. Although they are now supposed to be strictly protected, poachers from the towns have little difficulty in killing them. They are easily seen when the males are displaying. Special reserves have now been created for these really splendid birds in the Jaisalmer Desert National Park in Rajasthan and at Karera in Madhya

Pradesh. Even more scarce are their small relatives, the Bengal and Lesser Floricans, both of which are nearing extinction. The former is now restricted to the grasslands of the Nepalese *terai* and Assam and the latter to the Madhya Pradesh region, where I count myself lucky to have seen one.

In order to see wetlands birds, there is no better or more readily accessible locality than the magnificent reserve at Bharatpur in Rajasthan, now part of the Keoladeo Ghana National Park. Once the property of the local Maharajah, it earned fame for the enormous bags of ducks which were shot there. During two visits by British Viceroys the totals exceeded 4000 in a single day. Bharatpur is now justifiably world famous, offering an unrivalled spectacle of hundreds of thousands of ducks, herons, cranes, pelicans, storks, ibises, jacanas and other aquatic birds. No fewer than 360 species of birds have been identified in the reserve. They can be seen very easily, simply by walking along the *bunds* between the many ponds. Between July and October the trees and reed-beds are really crowded with nesting birds. The adjacent fields are alive with various plovers, peafowl, deer and antelopes. Some excellent ornithological research is being done there by the Bombay Natural History Society. Bharatpur is the only place in India where the ultra-rare western race of the Siberian Cranes still come every winter. Their flock, alas, has been reduced from 70 to only 37, possibly because some have been shot on migration at their resting place at the Abdi Estada Lake in Afghanistan, where the newly established wildlife reserve, which I had helped to create, collapsed in the conflict between Russian and Afghan troops. Fortunately a hitherto unknown population of the eastern race of this unique species has recently been discovered in China. All of India's crane species are also at risk to Pakistani crane-hunters, who sling lead-weighted cords at their passing migratory flocks.

Eight of the world's most magnificent pheasant species occupy the Himalayan region. Of these, the iridescent purple Impeyan and the Western Horned Tragopan are the most spectacular. All, unfortunately, are hunted by the hill tribes and are now increasingly difficult to find, although protective measures have been taken wherever they occur. The Pheasant Trust has been active in restoring populations by supplying eggs or young birds raised in Europe and both India and Pakistan now have captive-breeding projects for the rarer species.

The desert regions of the subcontinent are no less rewarding to ornithologists. Birds of prey of many kinds are numerous and can be seen feeding on the multitude of small rodents and lizards and on the plentiful carrion of domestic animals. There are always several species of sandgrouse around the water-holes and everywhere there are interesting larks, shrikes and wheatears. The occasional *jheels* (lakes) in the Pakistan desert regions are invariably crowded with wading birds of many species and often with rarities such as Flamingoes or the curious little stiff-tailed White-headed Ducks. The best place to see large numbers of Flamingoes, however, is at their huge breeding colonies on the salt lakes in the Great Rann of Kutch, although the journey to get there by camel or jeep over the sun-scorched flats is pretty arduous. Temperatures can exceed 45°C, and photography is impeded by the levitations of the mirage.

To the serious ornithologist nothing can be more frustrating than the task of trying to identify the confusing host of small warblers, the 'little brown jobs' as they are often disparagingly called, and the even more numerous babblers and laughing-thrushes, of which there are no fewer than 162 species inhabiting the subcontinent. India's most famous ornithologist and conservationist, my old friend Dr Sálim Ali, has shown that it requires ten volumes to describe and illustrate all the birds of the region. This book, therefore, can do no more than whet the appetite of the visitor.

The Cold-blooded Creatures

No attempt to describe the wildlife of the Indian subcontinent can ignore its crocodilians, snakes and other reptiles. Of the first mentioned there are three species – the blunt-nosed Mugger, or Marsh Crocodile, the thin-snouted, fish-eating Gharial and the larger sea-going Estuarine Crocodile. All used to be very numerous before the skin-traders got to work on them. Today they are far from plentiful and the Gharial has only just escaped extermination. Apart from the problem of the skin traders, the buried eggs of all the crocodilians are subject to heavy predation by monitor lizards, mongooses and many other animals. During the second World War I remember seeing Muggers by the dozen basking on the banks of many rivers in India and Pakistan. Now such a sight is rare, but there is still a reasonable population in a few protected areas and in the Nepalese *terai*. The Gharial survived only because of strenuous efforts by the Indian and Nepalese governments following a WWF-sponsored survey, which showed that this inoffensive crocodile was on the brink of extinction. Although sometimes attaining a length of seven metres, it never attacks humans. A breeding project on the Rapti River in the Royal Chitwan National Park in Nepal was financed by the Frankfurt Zoo. There are now five similar and outstandingly successful WWF projects in India, the largest being in Orissa. Many hundreds of young Gharials and Muggers have been raised from eggs taken in the wild and when they have attained a length of about 1½ metres have been released in the local rivers. Some have been fitted with collars bearing miniature radio transmitters, so that their movements and survival can be monitored. The big salt-water Estuarine Crocodile can occasionally be seen in the tidal creeks of the Ganges, Brahmaputra and Mahanadi rivers and in some Indian coastal waters. A sanctuary has been established for them at Bhittar Kanika in Orissa, while others have been reared successfully by the Madras Crocodile Bank.

There are said to be no fewer than 236 species or distinctive subspecies of snakes in the subcontinent. Many of these can be seen in comfort in the Madras Snake Park, which was created by Romulus Whitaker with the help of the World Wildlife Fund as an educational project. Nearly all are not only harmless but actually beneficial to man in controlling the vast rodent population. Without snakes, mongooses and owls, India might be unable to feed itself. Even now, according to a recent FAO report, rats consume a tonnage of stored grain every year equivalent to the total tonnage imported into India and Bangladesh under the various Foreign Aid and Famine Relief programmes. The export of snake skins was a lucrative business until 1968, when the total reached ten million. This very harmful trade has now been banned.

There are only two really big snakes, the common Rock Python and the rather rare Reticulated Python, both of which can reach a length exceeding seven metres and a weight of 115 kilograms. They are, of course, non-poisonous and kill their prey by crushing it in their powerful coils. Small mammals are their usual prey. I know of only one human, a small boy, being a victim; but pythons often seek shelter in the thatched roofs of village houses, where their discovery can cause much excitement. I did not realise just how powerful these beautifully marked snakes are until I was involved in catching one barely five metres long for examination in the Hill Tracts. It required four strong men to hold it relatively still before we released it into the jungle.

The venomous snakes are relatively few and some are strictly regional. These are the Common, Banded and Black Kraits, the Cobras (which occur in three forms – the Monocled, the Spectacled and the Black), the King Cobra, or Hamadryad, of the rain forests, (which can occasionally attain five metres in length,) the Russell's and Saw-scaled Vipers, the Coral Snakes, the Bamboo and Himalayan Pit Vipers and the various Sea Snakes, of which the Banded is the most common. None will deliberately attack humans unless provoked or accidentally stepped upon. Nevertheless, because 80 per cent of India's 750,000,000 people live bare-footed in villages where snakes are attracted to seek vermin or shelter in their mud houses, it is perhaps not surprising that nearly 9000 succumb every year to snake-bites. This horrifying figure has to be seen in proper perspective. Death and serious injury come in a multitude of guises to the poor in India. For example, it was recently reported that whereas only four people in Bombay were hospitalised for snake-bites in one year, no fewer than 20,000 were admitted with serious rat-bites, most of them children bitten while sleeping. And, of course, neither snake-bites nor rat-bites can compare with the an-nual slaughter on India's undisciplined roads, where, in spite of the relatively small number of vehicles, the death-rate is among the highest in the world. To quote a typical newspaper report of a traffic accident: 'Three of the occupants of the taxi were killed outright; the *seven other passengers* all suffered broken arms or legs.'

The general attitude towards snakes is ambivalent. Usually it is one of fear, yet few villagers willingly kill them. Cobras indeed are venerated in many parts of India. In Kerala, part of the village compound is often set aside for snake worship. At one religious festival a dozen Cobras may be extracted from their holes in the bunds around the paddyfields and after an elaborate ceremony of veneration are carefully returned unharmed. The handlers are also apparently unharmed, although no attempt is made to remove or milk the poison fangs of the snakes. To a Western observer it is an astonishing demonstration of religious conviction.

Lizards of many species abound in the dry regions and the attractive little spatula-toed geckos can be seen running about on the walls and ceilings even in town hotel bedrooms, where they feast on the abundant flies and months. Some much larger geckos and agamids inhabit the tropical forests and deserts. One such species became very familiar to British troops in the Burmese jungle during the war, when its incessant nocturnal cry of *'tuck-too'* infuriated exhausted men trying to sleep.

Strangely enough, although many Indian villagers regard snakes benevolently, some Moslems are terrified by the completely harmless lizards, agamids and geckos. In Cholistan I was solemnly warned that the attractively marked little Leopard Gecko was so deadly that not only its bite but its breath could kill a man. The villagers became almost hysterical when we handled one for photography. A small and equally harmless skink (a type of legless lizard) was described as a dangerous snake with a head at each end. Another lizard was accused of climbing up the legs of buffaloes to steal their milk, a superstition similar to that attributed in Europe to a bird, the Nightjar, or Goatsucker as it used to be called.

Several species of big monitor lizards, some nearly two metres in length, can be seen in both tropical forest and desert regions. My favourite is the black Ocellated Water Monitor, which is spangled with small yellow dots and has a long blue tongue which constantly flickers from its pink gape. It is a splendid sight basking on a log among the floating water hyacinths. An even more powerful creature is the fast-running Desert Monitor, which preys on rodents and birds in the Sind Desert. All the monitors, like the big snakes, have been constantly hunted by the skin traders, who exported their skins in hundreds of thousands for making handbags and shoes. As a consequence, all five monitor species are now listed as endangered and the export of their skins is prohibited.

Many different species of turtles can be seen around village ponds. Some grow to considerable size and are preyed upon by Jackals and other scavengers. In Nepal, Lammergeyer Vultures are known to pick them up and drop them on rocky ground in order to break their hard carapaces. It was probably one of these great birds which dropped a turtle on the head of the poet Aeschylus in Greece and killed him. In a pool in the Bayazid Bustami temple in Chittagong there are nearly 100 turtles of venerable age and astonishing size, which are locally regarded as sacred. They are fed every day on raw cow's lung, in which the enterprising street traders do a brisk trade with visiting pilgrims to the shrine. I was amused by the indignation of the pilgrims when hungry Black Kites and Jungle Crows swooped down and snatched the dripping hunks of meat from their hands before they could be offered to the turtles. The species is obscure, but is thought to be a giant race of the Black Pond Turtle of the Ganges region.

Throughout the world turtles are heavily exploited for their meat, eggs and carapaces or 'shells.' The State of Orissa, on India's east coast, has the distinction of preserving the breeding beaches of no fewer than 300,000 Olive Ridley Turtles, a species which elsewhere in the world is endangered. There are also colonies of Olive Ridley and Green Turtles on the sand beaches of some other States. A few Hawksbill Turtles nest in southern Tamil Nadu, in the Sundarbans and on offshore islands. In Pakistan the Sind Wildlife Management Board and the World Wildlife Fund protect important breeding beaches of Green and Olive Ridley Turtles at Hawkesbay and Sandspit, not far from Karachi. The local Pakistanis eat neither the eggs nor the meat of the turtles and their children have become enthusiastic helpers to the research team which supervises the colonies.

The Threatened Environment

From the preceding pages it will be obvious that throughout the Indian subcontinent wildlife has suffered a very serious decline, due chiefly to the enormous reduction of forests and the steep increase in the human and livestock populations. Nevertheless, the variety of species of mammals, birds, reptiles and plants which can still be enjoyed is astonishingly great. Some substantial remnants of all the various forest types still remain and the scenic splendour of the subcontinent, although much altered, is still magnificent. Moreover, thanks to the lead given by the heads of State of all the countries concerned, and particularly the example set by the late Mrs. Gandhi, there is now a firm and growing interest in the value of wildlife as a national heritage. Many State schools teach children to understand the importance of the natural world of living organisms and some universities have already produced graduates in environmental science and wildlife management. India now has many national parks and protected wildlife reserves which are attracting increasing numbers not only of foreign tourists but of local nationals. Protective legislation has been enacted and international agreements have been ratified for the protection of species and habitats. India and Nepal have joined the world-wide effort to create special Biosphere Reserves and have nominated potential sites. Steps have been taken to protect the 1000 species of wild orchids of the rain forests from the greed of commercial collectors. Bhutan, the least despoiled country and the one where wildlife has been least persecuted, has made an astonishing contribution by setting aside no less than 20 per cent of its territory as wildlife reserves. Nepal now has five excellent national parks and four wildlife reserves, while both Bangladesh and Pakistan, in spite of their now rather more limited resources of wildlife, also have vigorous conservation policies and many reserves. It might easily be concluded from all this that the corner has been turned and that the future for wildlife is bright.

Alas, such a conclusion would be wildly optimistic. The natural environment of the subcontinent, on which all life, including man, depends, is continuing to deteriorate at an alarming rate. To understand the reasons for this it is necessary to examine its present state and to consider the interaction of the various causes. These have recently been analysed with great frankness by a group of Indian scientists in a report published by the Centre for Science and the Environment. It was edited by Dr Anil Agarwal and entitled *A Citizen's Report on the State of the Indian Environment*. Most of the statistics in the following pages are quoted from this source.

First and foremost is the inescapable fact that the pressure of human numbers on the land and natural resources is rapidly increasing. India, with a population expected to reach one thousand million at the turn of the century, in spite of the progress of birth control, is already overcrowded. Bangladesh is one of the most densely populated countries in the world. Both countries, however, have sufficient potential or actual arable land and water to grow enough food to be self-supporting, yet both suffer from periodical famine. In a good year India is now self-sufficient in food, but hunger persists because of poverty and inequalities in distribution. Bangladesh is a nett importer of grain. It is not lack of natural resources but of adequately skilled management of the land and water which is at the root of the problem.

Both India and Pakistan have constructed major hydro-electric dams in order to provide increased energy and irrigation, but according to the *Citizen's Report* the results have been little short of catastrophic because they were not planned or executed in consultation with either qualified soil scientists or ecologists. In consequence, one quarter of India's 40,000,000 hectares of canal-irrigated land is now suffering from serious water-logging and silta-

tion. Most of the catchment areas have suffered a massive loss of topsoil and are turning into deserts which hundreds of thousands of peasant farmers have had to abandon. I saw clear evidence of this at the Kali River Dam in Karnataka and at the Tanbela Dam in Pakistan. The loss of tree-cover at Tarbela caused an annual loss of 400,000,000 tons of silt into the Indus River. Another ecological disaster is likely to be caused by the new Farakka barrage, which is diverting water from the Ganges in Bangladesh to India. Even long-established wildlife reserves have not escaped the ambitions of the engineers, who did not hesitate to flood the Ramganga Valley in the beautiful Corbett National Park in the Siwalik Hills, thus depriving the wild Elephant population of its feeding ground. There is now a proposal to construct a dam in the middle of the Manas Tiger Reserve, one of the most valuable wildlife areas in the subcontinent. Such proposals are heart-breaking to the devoted officials responsible for conservation.

In India the amount of land subject to flooding has doubled in the last ten years. Dams which the engineers had calculated would be fully effective for 100 years are now expected to fail in only 30 or 40 years because of miscalculations of the rate of siltation. Many African countries have paid similar penalties to the lure of grandiose but ill-planned hydro-electric projects financed by the World Bank. Jawaharlal Nehru called those in India 'the temples of modern India as testimonials to human toil and skill.' Toil, yes, but so far as skill is concerned this veneration must be judged against the penalties paid in rural areas, which have frequently far outweighed the value of the extra power generated. Comparison with China is illuminating: although China has suffered severely from ecological mismanagement, it has constructed many thousands of small dams, which now provide one third of the nation's electric power, with a minimum of the land damage which so often follows the building of gigantic dams.

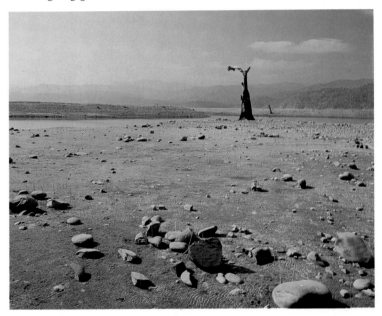

The dam constructed on the Ramganga river has had a drastic impact on the wildlife in Corbett National Park. Besides drowning a large area of forest, it has dislocated the migratory route of elephant herds.

It has been calculated that 53 per cent of India's land is now subject to serious degradation from erosion, waterlogging, salinity, alkalinity, or the ill-effects of shifting cultivation. Of these, flooding and excessive salinity are the chief problems and both can be attributed to inadequate control of the major rivers. Pollution is another very serious problem. No less than 70 per cent of all available freshwater sources in India are now polluted. The use of chemical fertilizers and pesticides is encouraged by the government. But the factories discharge their untreated effluents into the rivers and the payment of subsidies encourages the overdosing of crops, so that the run-off quickly pollutes the irrigation channels. The factories are all too often located close to big towns where labour is readily available, the consequence of which was demonstrated by the recent tragedy at Bhopal, where 2500 inhabitants were killed by a gas leakage from a Union Carbide factory. The multi-national chemical companies of the United States and Europe, where lethal and persistent products such as DDT, Aldrin and BHC are now banned by law, still cynically export them to the Third World and great quantities of them are used in the Indian subcontinent. Sulphur-dioxide and oxides of nitrogen as a fall-out from factory chimneys in the form of 'acid rain' is also damaging public health, forests and treasured buildings such as the Taj Mahal. Many once famous sand beaches of India, which represented potential sources of wealth from tourism, are now hopelessly spoiled by the back-wash of industrial pollutants and human excreta. Even the marine national park on the Gulf of Kutch, which was once a paradise for marine life, is threatened by spillage from an oil refinery.

The greatest cause of pollution, however, is not inorganic chemicals but the fact that one third of India's town dwellers and 99 per cent of its rural population have no sanitary facilities whatever. Out of 3119 towns and cities, only eight have fully adequate sewerage systems. *A Citizens Report* states that human waste accounts for four times as much water pollution as all the industrial and agricultural effluents combined. It quotes the example of the Yamuna River. Before this river enters Delhi (which has quadrupled its population in only 20 years) it is reasonably pure, with only 7500 coliform organisms per 100 millilitres, of water. Below Delhi it contains 24 million per 100 millilitres, and is nothing but a lifeless sewer covered with dead fish. Water-borne diseases such as dysentery, typhoid, jaundice, cholera, filariasis and guinea-worm are rampant and many are actually increasing. Three children die from such diseases or from malnutrition in India every minute. Mosquitoes and sandflies have bred immunity to the government's massive use of DDT spraying and in consequence the scourge of malaria has again increased sharply during the past decade. A national programme aimed ultimately at a complete sewerage system is now planned by the government, but already fears are expressed that although this will help city dwellers it is very unlikely to alleviate the problem in rural areas where the great majority of the population lives.

Outsiders who know and love India, as I do, are always puzzled by the difference between the insistence, at all levels of society, on the scrupulous daily ablutions of the body and the almost total lack of concern about the disposal of human excreta. Our Western preoccupation with hygiene is looked upon as not only ridiculously fastidious, but as uneconomic, if not barbarous. Every day throughout most of Asia hundreds of millions of people squat unconcernedly to defecate at the roadside and in the paddyfields as their ancestors have always done. The village pond serves not only for bathing, washing clothes and watering cattle, but in innumerable cases also as a source of water for drinking and cooking – and as a cess-pit for the spread of disease. Drinking-water from a stand-pipe is available in a very small percentage of villages, but it functions only erratically and sometimes not at all.

The beautiful yet pernicious water hyacinth, *Eichornia crassipes,* **is the scourge of fresh-water systems throughout the subcontinent.**

India has 237,000,000 domestic cattle including buffaloes, and 50,000,000 goats and sheep. Less than a quarter of the 3,000,000,000 tons of manure they produce every year goes back to the land. The rest is dried and burnt as fuel. Yet, above all, the land cries out for organic fertilisation. Millions of tons of water hyacinths choke every village pond and 4,000,000 hectares of India's waterways.

These beautiful but invasive plants were introduced from South America and are capable of multiplying 60,000 times in only eight months. They offer a limitless source of free fertiliser but remain unused except for making paper, or for feeding pigs, which are surely misplaced priorities. India's farmers rarely learn the value of ploughing back either manure or vegetable waste from crops, yet their crops deplete the soil of nearly 18,000,000 tons of plant nutrients every year, so the land inevitably becomes steadily less productive. Even if the farmers realise this, the pernicious practice by the land-owners of moving their tenants from area to area on a share-cropping basis is sufficient to kill any interest in soil improvement. Even in Punjab, once famous as 'the green revolution State' which achieved the highest yield of wheat in the subcontinent, too much is being taken out of the soil and too little put back. Today Punjab is listed as having one of the lowest levels of plant nutrients in its land, yet 5,000,000 tons of nutrient-rich rice straw are burnt there every year, instead of being ploughed back.

The fact that cows are sacred to Hindus poses yet another problem. Nearly all of them are emaciated and disease ridden, but on religious grounds may not be culled. Millions of them forage for what they can find in the forests, deserts or city streets, where they cause countless accidents. Motorists who run into them risk a lynching. As beef is 'unclean' to so many, their value to the national economy is in any case very small. Nehru, who knew the weaknesses of the Indian character better than anyone, said:

'In India there is a difference between precept and practice. In no country is life valued in theory so much as in India and many people hesitate to destroy even the meanest or most harmful of animals. But in practice we ignore the animal world. We grow excited about the protection of the cow . . . But we imagine we have done our duty by passing some legislation. This results not in the protection of the cow but in much harm to it as well as to human beings. The cattle are let loose and deteriorate, so that the very purpose for which we value them is defeated.'

This confusion between precept and practice is at the root of many of India's problems. The government is unquestionably humanitarian and strives mightily to improve the lot of its people. India's scientists are among the best in the world and there is certainly no lack of knowledge either of what is wrong, or of the means by which improvements could be made. Yet again and again priorities seem to be muddled and the fulfilment of admirable plans gets lost or diverted in the world's largest and most pervasive bureaucracy. Although the need for improved sanitation and wiser land-use policies is everywhere admitted, priority was given to the costly development of the atomic bomb, which most people believe few countries needed less than India. The plight of the rural population, of which 350 million are living at below the recognised subsistence level, is obvious to all, but it is usually the comparatively well-off city dwellers who most benefit from government policies. India rightly takes pride in its claim to be the world's greatest democracy, but so long as the caste system persists, with its pernicious effects on political, social and economic life, it is difficult to see how the difference between precept and practice will ever be overcome. For all the government's benevolent intentions, to the peasant farmer even the lowliest official has a terrifying, almost god-like power over his existence. Every villager is acutely aware that unless he has the means to bribe an official his complaints will never be heard, let alone be considered.

When Mahatma Gandhi promised that there would be no high class and no low class in India he was wildly applauded. Yet 36 years later the caste system can still be seen at every level of society. Very few Westerners can comprehend its intricate ramifications, or the depth of the conviction which sustains it. The cultured Brahmin who feels polluted if touched by an 'untouchable,' suffers from it just as much as the poorest vagrant who is forbidden the use of the village well and must drink at the cattle pond. Voluntary efforts to improve the lot of the landless and illiterate 'scheduled people' are still often resented by villagers, on the grounds that the destitute should not be encouraged to compete with their betters. Local courts have frequently supported this view. The in-bred, patient acceptance of the caste system, which the Mahatma tried so hard to break, is something which village co-operatives and well-meaning government relief programmes for the poor can alleviate, but the problem itself remains intractable. India remains firmly compartmentalised by caste and religion.

So far as the natural environment is concerned, it is not too late to reverse many of the adverse trends from which the subcontinent is suffering. Legislation already exists for the control of pollution, although it is rarely implemented. Europe and America have demonstrated that it is possible to restore the purity of water sources by the strict enforcement of such legislation. It would be possible to restore the soil fertility of many agricultural areas if the huge resources of organic waste and animal manure were ploughed back instead of going up in smoke and if erosion by wind and water were better controlled. Techniques now exist for halting the disastrous spread of deserts, many of which in Pakistan and north-west India were once forested. The degradation of forests by fuel gatherers could be alleviated if governments developed and subsidised efficient bio-gas cookers for rural villages and ensured that supplies of wet cattle dung were equitably shared to fuel them. In 1982 fewer than 20,000 such cookers existed in India (compared with 7,000,000 in China) and unless a family owned five or more cows it had insufficient manure to produce any methane gas for the cooker. Only 10 per cent of the rural poor own as many cattle as this, so the cookers failed to get the support they deserved. There is also ample waste-land available for planting quick-growing trees to supplement fuel and building supplies, if this were done on a large enought scale and under government subsidy with the active co-operation of rural villages. A notably successful example of this already exists in Gujarat State and there is certainly no lack of expertise in India's very efficient Forest Department.

A considerable variation in the attitudes of State Governments towards matters such as these made it difficult to bring about the coherent national conservation strategy for which Mrs. Gandhi was striving. Nevertheless some notable progress has been made. For example, in order to control the increasing losses of forested areas, which between 1950 and 1980 had amounted to 4,300,000 hectares, the Forest (Conservation) Act of 1980 was introduced. This immediately prevented any State Government or other authority from diverting forest land to non-forestry purposes without the prior consent of the Central Government. Although considered controversial at the time, this Act has been highly beneficial.

India now has only 14 per cent of its original forests left; Bangladesh has a mere 9 per cent, while only 6 per cent of Pakistan's huge land is forested. Between 1951 and 1972 nearly 3,500,000 hectares of native forest were felled in India and by 1982 the rate of loss had accelerated to more than a million hectares a year including bamboo and mangrove forests. Some extensive replanting is, of course, being done, but most of this is of commercial tree species which do not provide the fruit, nuts, foliage, resins and thatching which are so essential to forest tribes as well as to wildlife. In the past 30 years the total area of replanting amounted to just over 3,000,000 hectares, but less than 20 per cent of this was intended for soil or moisture conservation. In Bihar State, where owing to failure in communication tribal people resisted the government policy of replacing virgin forest with commercial trees, there was serious rioting, resulting in 13 deaths and 200 arrests. The government failed to recognise that the great majority of its millions of primitive tribal people are totally dependent on the produce of the natural forest for their livelihood.

That grass-root support for environmental reform concerning the use of forests would be forthcoming from the rural population has been demonstrated by the success of the Chipko Andolan movement. Beginning in the Garhwal Himalayas as a local tree-hugging protest against the destruction of natural forests, this rapidly became a substantial and widely publicised native-tree planting campaign led by the Chipko women. Their tree seedlings were carefully nurtured and are said to have achieved a much higher rate of both survival and growth than in the neighbouring government-controlled monoculture plantations. The Chipko movement has been internationally acclaimed.

Sufficient expertise exists in the world to make safer and more productive use of the subcontinent's ample resources of water. According to the FAO even Bangladesh could be made self-supporting in food if its irrigation and agriculture were modernised. But mechanized farming is not the answer. This benefits only the large land-owner and deprives the poor of their traditional labour-intensive employment as weeders, reapers and threshers of cereal crops. Foreign Aid should be concentrated on encouraging self-help and on providing expertise to improve the use of local resources, rather than on the present export of government-subsidised surplus grain from the West. Whether such reforms will take place will depend largely on the wisdom of the governments concerned. But also on the manner in which the Foreign Aid Programmes of the Western governments are devised. At present most of them are far from altruistic in their insistence on a *quid pro quo*. 'I'll send you grain if you will buy my tractors,' is scarcely humanitarian. The United Nations, the World Bank and the International Monetary Fund are at last trying to overcome this horse-trading attitude which inflicts such unnecessary hardship on recipient countries. At the United Nations the environmental crisis which threatens the subcontinent is very fully documented. What is lacking is the political will to take the necessary action while there is yet time to avert catastrophe.

Mrs Gandhi used to declare that India must stand on its own feet, by which she meant that it must solve its own problems and not depend on foreign aid. This brave posture deserves commendation. A similar determination can be seen in Nepal, which is one of the poorest nations in the world and heavily dependent on its natural resources for survival. No less than 87 per cent of its energy resources are provided by burning wood from its forests. The resultant massive deforestation has led to serious erosion and flooding, which affects not only Nepal but also India and Bangladesh. Recognising this, HM King Birendra called for a national conservation strategy, which is being devised with the help of the International Union for Conservation of Nature and Natural Resources. It coordinates long-term environmental planning with strategies for population control and industrialisation and is supported by a national educational programme concerning the need to protect the environment and wildlife. It is a very great step forward. Nepal is one of the first countries to have responded so whole-heartedly to the recommendations of the World Conservation Strategy, which were launched in 1980 by the IUCN, the WWF and the United Nations Environment Programme (UNEP). By adopting a policy of complete co-ordination between *all* government activities which have a bearing on the fate of the natural environment, Nepal is setting an example to the world. Although most nations now take environmental matters seriously, even the United Kingdom and the United States still suffer from the often competing ambitions of their various government ministries. If a problem happens to have a bearing on the short-term national economy it is usually this factor rather than the environmental consequence which has the ultimate sanction. Only the adoption of a firmly-held and fully co-ordinated national conservation strategy can overcome such conflicts.

So far as the future for wildlife in the Indian subcontinent is concerned, I have nothing but admiration for the measures already taken in the face of such overpowering local problems. Even Afghanistan, which I last visited with HRH The Duke of Edinburgh on behalf of the World Wildlife Fund just before the Russian invasion, had by then created wildlife reserves. Whether in the long term the measures taken in the subcontinent will remain effective will, I believe, depend on what Indian experts are already calling a better understanding of the human dimension in wildlife management. By this they mean the integration of local people into the conservation planning, by identifying wildlife and wilderness areas as essential elements of a resource system in a socio-economic sense. Unless this can be achieved there is a danger that the conservation of wildlife will increasingly be regarded as putting the welfare of wild animals before that of people. In countries where a great percentage of the population lives at mere subsistence level it is to be expected that such antagonism could easily arise.

Some valuable studies have been conducted in India by comparing two different methods of handling the human equation when setting up wildlife reserves. One was at the Gir Lion Reserve in Gujarat, the other at the Palamau Tiger Reserve in Bihar. In the former it was decided to remove all the Maldhari villagers and their cattle and resettle them beyond the reserve boundaries. They were given fresh, unpolluted land which was ploughed at government expense. Free transportation, essential building and agricultural equipment, water resources, a school and a community centre were provided. The re-location was highly successful and achieved without social protest. The cost worked out at less than $US 250 a head, plus a similar amount as a loan for house-building. As described earlier in this book, the effect of the removal of the Maldharis and their huge herds of cattle was immediately apparent in the reserve. With the recovery of the vegetation and the sowing of the old village sites with native grasses, the populations of deer and other animals quickly recovered. Nevertheless, the operation, although so successfully handled, did nothing to interest the villagers in the conservation objectives, nor to integrate them in the project in a socio-economic sense.

At Palamau a different approach was used. A fully protected core area for wildlife was established, but the tribal Bihari villagers were permitted, within certain limits, to remain in the substantial buffer zone around the reserve. In this they continued to graze their cattle and to harvest controlled quantities of their traditional necessities such as bamboo, thatching grass, wood fuel and wild fruit, roots and tubers for food. A limited amount of shifting cultivation in marginal areas was also permitted. Moreover the tribal people were employed in the construction of patrol roads, guard huts, watch towers, fire-breaks and other necessary work in the reserve. Their interest in the conservation programme became obvious and they benefited from the additional water sources which were developed for the wildlife. By this integration into the management planning, both goodwill and sustained and active co-operation were obtained and all social disruption avoided.

A Malasar tribal village in the heart of the Anaimalai Sanctuary in the Western Ghats. Tribals in India have traditionally lived in close harmony with the indigenous forests, and any threat to this vulnerable environment poses a consequential threat to their whole way of life.

The Indian Department of the Environment, which has now been taken into the Prime Minister's office, has these and similar case histories on which to base future planning. It would appear that the full integration of often illiterate tribal people into the conservation effort is not only desirable but completely achievable. It should go far in overcoming the threat of a man versus animals conflict. In this respect India has again pioneered an admirable example to the rest of Asia.

I have always been fascinated by my occasional contacts with the aboriginal tribes which I have met in Asia, South America, Australasia and Central Africa. Unlike civilised societies, they have learned to live in easy equilibrium with the natural world; their reliance on the resources of the forests or deserts which they inhabit is always deeply impressive. Such people are completely remote, having absolutely nothing in common with the Western world. The forest tribes of India are no exception. Everything they need for

survival is found in the bountiful forests and forest streams. There are ample sources of food, bamboos for building, palm leaves for thatching, vines for binding and they know of countless medicinal plants for their ailments. They never plunder or abuse the rich generosity of the forests, nor kill any living thing wantonly.

Now many of the Indian forest tribes are being dispossessed by the felling of their forests and are being driven out into the alien world of officialdom, incomprehensible laws and customs which frighten them. Unable to cope with the traumatic confusion of the twentieth century, they are deeply unhappy. What, for example, is to become of the 75,000 Madia Gonds who are being dispossessed of their tribal land in order that hydro-electric installations may be built on the Godavari River? Or the displaced Cholanaickans of Kerala State who have taken to a troglodyte existence, to the embarrassment of local officials who find them almost impossible to assimilate? The future of the 'Scheduled Tribes,' as they are called, poses many problems for the Government and as they number some 44,000,000 throughout India, there are no easy answers.

During construction of Karnataka's Kabini dam, Kurba tribals were translocated from their valley settlements to regions close by, where large tracts of indigenous forest were cleared for their benefit. Destruction of forests in the subcontinent today poses a serious ecological threat to the whole environment.

Throughout its long history, India has demonstrated its genius for quietly assimilating many widely differing peoples, and unique skill in overcoming the seemingly insurmountable social problems which some have temporarily caused. A part of the tribal population has already been educated and some have even occupied positions of responsibility in local government. It will take time to assimilate the remainder, but time has always been on India's side. All the past assimilations have enriched the nation's culture and the Scheduled Tribes will undoubtedly make their contribution. It is already recognized that the forest tribals have unique knowledge and skill in the use of medicinal plants, which can benefit not only India but the world at large. This opportunity is being actively pursued and encouraged by the United Nations agencies such as the World Health Organization.

The natural world of the Indian subcontinent is now at the crossroads. Either the governments of the countries concerned will recognize the reality of the present threats to the environment and make a concerted effort to overcome them, or they will have to face the loss of much of their natural heritage and increasing hardship for their people. Almost all the causes of the sickness from which the environment is suffering have had their counterparts in other countries. They have been studied in depth and have been fully documented by experts of many nations. Scientists in India and its neighbouring countries are fully alive to the need for urgent action, as has been demonstrated by the conclusions expressed in the *Citizens Report*. Its findings echoed those relating to the region in the *Global 2000 Report*, a world-wide environmental survey commissioned by former President Jimmy Carter and prepared by a team of distinguished specialists. There is no mystery about the nature of the reforms needed to arrest the present adverse trends, which are making Man himself an endangered species. Two things are required. First, fully co-ordinated national conservation strategies which combine eco-development on a sustained-yield basis with long-term objectives for agriculture, forestry, industry, public health and population control. Second, a new set of planning and financial priorities, which place the welfare of the natural environment and people above all other considerations. Both would require great political determination. It is, of course, easy enough to suggest solutions, but to implement them is another matter. To create the necessary governmental infra-structure alone would be a task of daunting proportions.

Far from playing a passive role in the face of impending disaster, the Indian Government has continually strengthened its conservation measures, often despite strong opposition by vested interests. Almost unique in the world is the Indian Constitution, which lays down as a Principle of State Policy that 'it shall be the duty of every citizen to protect and improve the natural environment, including forests, lakes, rivers and wildlife and to have compassion for all living creatures.' The Indian Board for Wildlife, which advises both Central and State Governments on matters relating to conservation, is headed by the Prime Minister in person. Since 1970, the efficacy of this arrangement has been amply demonstrated. In 1972 the Wildlife Protection Act was passed, providing a central legal framework for controlling hunting and all trade in wildlife and wildlife products. In 1973 'Project Tiger' was implemented. This led to the creation of 15 protected reserves totalling 25,000 square kilometres. Although originally regarded as a single-species project, it was in effect a total ecosystem preservation which benefitted all forms of wildlife and was one of the most successful ever executed by any country. In 1976 a Directorate of Wildlife Education and Research was established, providing post-graduate diploma courses in wildlife management. This was followed by the creation of the Wildlife Institute of India, which established a strong professional and scientific base for conservation.

Unlike many prominent nations, India has ratified all the main international conservation conventions: the Convention on International Trade in Endangered Species of Flora and Fauna (CITES); the Convention on Wetlands of International Importance (the Ramsar Convention); the Convention on Migratory Species of Wild Animals (the Migratory Species Convention) and the International Convention for the Regulation of Whaling (the Whaling Convention). The driving force behind these initiatives was the indefatigable Indira Gandhi. She played a leading role in the launching of the World Conservation Strategy in Stockholm and immediately introduced it in India. In 1983 the historic National Wildlife Action Plan was adopted with the full backing of all the States and Union Territories, thus implementing the resolutions passed at the World Parks Congress in Bali and at the UN General Assembly on the World Charter for Nature. Finally, India now has no fewer than 52 National Parks and 223 well-managed wildlife reserves of various kinds. Such a record puts many other nations to shame.

The natural world is the result of millions of years of infinitely gradual evolution, which in the Indian sub-continent was abundantly expressed in terms of scenic splendour and variety of living organisms at the turn of the twentieth century. The decline which became apparent by the middle of the century is now becoming rapidly steeper. Every year that passes sees more irreparable losses which make salvation more difficult. Future generations will not forgive us if this magnificent world heritage is not saved for posterity. It is not sufficient merely to hope that it will somehow be saved by local initiative. It is part of our threatened world and its fate is our fate.

It will be said, with justice, that someone from the West, which consumes four-fifths of the natural resources of the world, has no right to criticise policies or conditions in the Indian subcontinent. It is, however, certainly not by right but with humility and I hope with objectivity that my views, as seen through Western eyes, are expressed. I can only hope that my friends in the various countries concerned will understand my anxiety, as a conservationist, about the future for a part of the world for whose gentle and long-suffering people I have unbounded admiration.

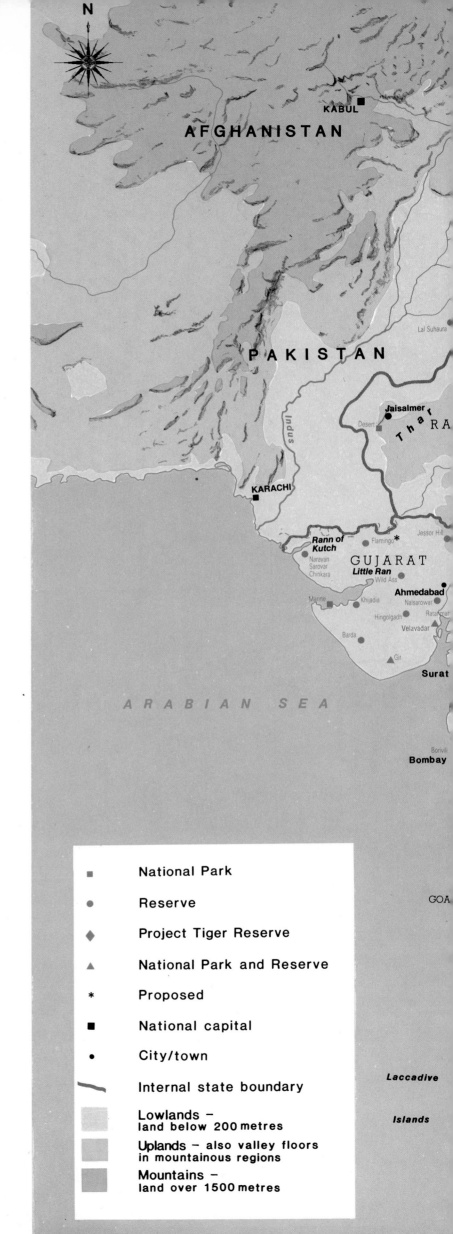

■	National Park
●	Reserve
◆	Project Tiger Reserve
▲	National Park and Reserve
*	Proposed
■	National capital
●	City/town
⌒	Internal state boundary
	Lowlands – land below 200 metres
	Uplands – also valley floors in mountainous regions
	Mountains – land over 1500 metres

JAMMU

CHINA

Karakoram

K2
(8611)▲

AND

Leh

KASHMIR

●Srinagar

LAMABAD■

TIBET

●Amritsar

HIMACHAL
PRADESH

PUNJAB

Simla●

CHANDIGARH

Himalaya

HARYANA

Delhi●

■NEW DELHI Rampur

Desert

Indus

Annapurna
(8078)▲

Mt. Everest
(8848)▲

Gangtok
■THIMPHU

ARUNACHAL
PRADESH

●Jaipur

UTTAR PRADESH

Agra●

KATHMANDU■

Kanchenjunga
(8586)▲

SIKKIM

BHUTAN

●Dibrugarh

●Itanagar

STHAN

●Lucknow

N E P A L

Ghaghara

Gauhati

ASSAM

NAGALAND

dhpur

●Kanpur

Yamuna

Patna●

Ganga

●Kohima

MEGHALAYA

●Shillong

MANIPUR

●Imphal

●Varanasi

BIHAR

BANGLADESH

RISTHAN

MADHYA

●Bhopal

Agartala●

MIZORAM

●Aizawl

DACCA■

TRIPURA

Narmada

●Jabalpur

WEST

Vindhya Range

PRADESH

Setpura Range

BENGAL

Howrah● ●Calcutta

Tapti

Nagpur●

Raipur●

●Chittagong

I N D I

A

ORISSA

Mouths of the Ganges

BURMA

MAHARASHTRA

●Bhubaneswar

Godavari

Deccan

●Poona

Krishna

●Hyderabad

●Sholapur

ANDHRA

Ghats

Eastern

●Vishakhapatnam

Ghats

BAY OF BENGAL

RANGOON

●Kurnool

PRADESH

KARNATAKA

Western

Ghats

Andaman
Islands

ngalore

●Bangalore

●Madras

●Mysore

TAMIL

NADU

●Cochin

KERALA

●Madurai

Point Calimere

SRI LANKA

Reserves set up to protect particular species:

Project Tiger Reserves
Manas
Palamau
Bandipur
Wayanaad
Periyar
Kanha
Indravati
Melghat
Simlipal NP
Sariska
Ranthambhor
Mudamalai
Corbett
Dudhwa
Buxa
Namdapha

Bird Reserves
Nelpattu
Flamingo
Nalsarowar
Khijadia
Sultanpur
Ranganathittoo
Peruvannamuzhy
Ghatigaon (Bustard)
Kerera (Bustard)
Karnala
Bharatpur (Keoladeo Ghana)
Vedanthangal
Point Calimere

Other sanctuaries
primarily for an
endangered species

Blackbuck:
Pranahita
Velavadar
Ranebennur
Talchhappar

Gharial:
Chambal
Raneh Fall
Son River
Satkosia Gorge

Lion:
Barda
Gir

Wild Ass:
Wild Ass

Sloth Bear:
Dumkhar

Gaur:
Radhanagari

Chinkara:
Narayan Sarovar
Chinkara

●Trivandrum

OCEAN

0   km   500

The Himalayas
The Edge of the Roof of the World

In the intense, sub-zero silence of the sky at an altitude of 9000 metres, a solitary Himalayan Griffon Vulture rides the wind. Far below, between the shreds of cloud blown like smoke among the high peaks, it can see the glistening ice slopes, plunging to the chaotically shattered lips of the glaciers. Below them again sprawl the vast stony barrens, where Marmots pop in and out of their burrows and Snow Partridges scratch for fallen seed among the rocks.

The barrens in turn fall away southwards to the stunted birches, then the taller conifers, and finally the deep gorges, dark with rhododendron forest, where a thousand streams cascade down the rocks. Only a few kilometres beyond that, as the altitude diminishes, the Nepalese foothills give way to the vivid green of the semi-tropical *terai* and then the luxuriant and humid tropical deciduous jungle of the Indian States of Uttar Pradesh and Bihar.

The transition through so many different climatic and vegetational zones over a distance of less than a hundred kilometres is dramatic. To the north of the Himalayas is the immense and inhospitable Tibetan Plateau, but to the east and west, in an unbroken succession of snowy peaks, the Himalayan range extends for 3000 kilometres, at either end curving southwards towards Afghanistan and Burma. With 50 mountain peaks exceeding 7600 metres in altitude, they form one of the world's greatest mountain chains. Soaring above them is Mount Everest, or Sagarmatha, Goddess Mother of the World, as the Nepalese call it, with a height of 8848 metres. The only passes through this barrier, the ancient trade routes to the icy, windswept roof of the world in Tibet and China, involve climbing to an altitude of at least 5500 metres.

The Himalayas form a weather barrier which is responsible for India's monsoon climate. Three of the world's greatest rivers, the Indus, the Ganges and the Brahmaputra, rise among its peaks and flow southward to water the heat-stricken northern plains of Pakistan and India, where 15 per cent of the world's population depends upon them for survival.

The alpine region of the Himalayas abounds with colourful flowers of incomparable beauty. The famous Valley of Flowers in the Garhwal Himal affords an easy means of seeing them. The stony alpine regions of the Himalayas above the tree-line are carpeted in spring with colourful cushions of blue gentians and starred with saxifrages, asters, anemones, primulas, fritillarias and yellow edelweiss. Junipers and buckthorns cling to the stony slopes.

Lower down, in the alpine forests of birch and conifers, are immense thickets of rhododendrons, some growing up to 20 metres high. Among them are laurels, huge white magnolias, pink daphnes, azaleas, various lilies and the famous blue, yellow and crimson Himalayan poppies. Fragrant white Himalayan musk roses climb to the tops of the trees.

Up above the tree-line, only the occasional accumulated litter of a climbers' camp defaces the scene – evidence that man has dared to challenge the heights. Below, the presence of man is more evident. Here and there are isolated Buddhist monasteries with their picturesque stupas and fluttering white prayer flags. Then come the Sherpa villages, where shaggy yaks shelter in the lower rooms of snug, stone-built houses. Increasingly, the natural vegetation has been lopped for fuel or removed to make way for cultivation. Even the spectacular Khumbu National Park has its legacy of trees mutilated by trekking parties.

In only ten years Nepal has lost one third of its magnificent forests. Most of the foothills have been stripped bare and everywhere there are intricate stone terraces, created by superhuman effort, for the growing of millet, barley, maize and potatoes. Potatoes are grown by the Sherpas of Nepal up to an altitude of 5800 metres. However, many of the centuries-old terraces have long ago been eroded and abandoned because of the loss of the stabilizing tree-cover. From the air the sheer extent of this monument to the frailty of human endeavour is a saddening if fascinating sight. The loss of trees has resulted in countless landslides, some of which have destroyed whole villages. The higher the terracing, the greater the landslides.

Despite the losses, however, there is still a wealth of interest for the botanist. In a single day more than a hundred species of birds can be seen. Such spectacular animals as Snow Leopards, Black Bears, Red Pandas and various mountain sheep and goats roam the heights of Gilgit, Hunza, Ladakh, Nepal, Sikkim and Bhutan. Although hunters of many nations have taken a heavy toll of these animals in the past, the governments of all the Himalayan countries have in recent years made strenuous efforts to protect them.

A chain of National Parks and Wildlife Reserves now stretches from the Khunjerab in Pakistan, past the superb Khumbu National Park surrounding Everest, to the reserves of Sikkim, Bhutan and Assam, where mountain wildlife and stupendous scenery can be enjoyed to the full. Access to those at high altitudes is limited by snowy conditions, but the others are readily accessible in the dry season and provide facilities for visitors. To see them is to enjoy the experience of a lifetime, but whereas there was once a long slow trek up from the Indian plains, the modern traveller, arriving by air, may take some time to acclimatise to the high altitudes. The little Momblasa, or Everest View, Lodge at Khumjung, perched high above the Sherpa village of Namche Bazar and the Dudh Kosi gorge, has oxygen masks available in every bedroom. The hotel balconies offer magnificent panoramic views of the peaks of Everest, Lhotse, Nuptse and Ama Dablam. Tourists who have jumped by helicopter direct from Kathmandu often have to go straight to bed with an oxygen mask, missing the chance to enjoy their surroundings. However, this can be avoided by trekking in easy stages from Kathmandu, by way of Namche, up to the 4000 metre altitude of the lodge.

The Shang Valley in Ladakh, at an altitude of 4000 metres.

Above: The arid slopes of the Karakoram range rise above the fertile strip that borders the upper Indus.

Far left: Bharal, or Blue Sheep, in typical semi-desert habitat on mountain slopes, high above the Shang valley in Ladakh. Bharal are also found in the high, windswept barrens of Tibet, Nepal and Sikkim. In summer they live at altitudes of up to 5500 metres, descending to about 3500 metres in winter. Neither sheep nor goat, though having some resemblance to both, their horns are smooth and swept back like those of a goat, though the rams are not bearded. A Bharal climbs with goat-like agility, but its flocks graze like sheep – invariably on open slopes, and avoiding bushy or forested areas. Bharal are extremely alert and difficult to approach. They are preyed upon by Snow Leopards, which lie in wait for them among the rocks.

Left: An immature Bharal ram. When adult, its horns will sweep backwards in a semi-circle. The slate-grey coloration provides splendid camouflage on rocky mountain slopes.

Right: Although the Himalayan peaks in Ladakh are not as high as in Nepal, they are still awe-inspiring. The mountains are equally rugged, with similarly immense glaciers descending their slopes from the high snow fields. (Left and right foreground.) In summer their melting waters create spectacular waterfalls which cascade into the valleys far below.

The Himalayan range is nearly 3000 kilometres long and 200 kilometres wide, forming an almost impregnable barrier between the Indian subcontinent and Tibet and China. The northern side, known as the Great Himalaya, lies along the edge of the Tibetan Plateau and has an average height of 6000 metres. The mountains were formed by a violent crumbling and up-thrust of the earth's crust along the edge of the Central Asian tableland, beginning in the Miocene period. The range is still rising and moving northwards under the pressure of the Indian peninsula, which once formed part of the super-continent of Gondwanaland before drifting on the earth's molten crust to join the Asian land mass.

The animal life of the Himalayas is specially adapted to the fierce winds and extreme cold of the high altitudes. All the mammals have undercoats of dense fur and their feet are well adapted to travel through snow and over ice-clad rocks. The Yak's long, woolly coat and bushy tail, which reach almost to the ground, help to keep its feet warm in winter. Some of the small animals such as Marmots and Mouse Hares, which live as high as 5500 metres, store food in their burrows and, like the bears, go into a state of hibernation in the coldest weather. Other animals descend to the tree line. Langur Monkeys manage to survive at 3700 metres, and even Tigers have left their tracks in the snow at nearly 4000 metres. Some birds, such as Snow Finches and the hardy Snow Partridge, spend almost their entire lives on or above the snow line, and some even nest in the intense cold at 5000 metres.

Right: The trunk road from Kashmir to Ladakh crosses heavily eroded sandstone formations above the tree line. The barren slopes are cut by deep gorges.

Left: The Suru Valley in Ladakh. Still above the tree line, but here the stony slope is green with alpine vegetation. Above it rise the twin peaks of Nun (7725 m) and Kun (7672 m).

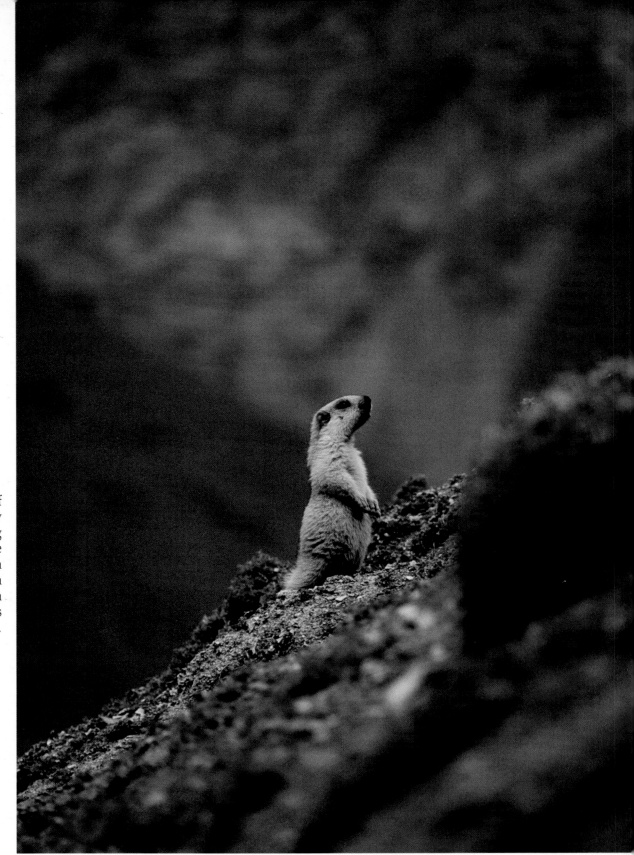

Right and far right: Colonies of Himalayan Marmots occupy the rocky slopes at very high altitudes, making their homes in burrows which give these perky animals some protection from the eagles which prey upon them. Ever-watchful, they stand on their hind legs and warn their fellows with a shrill whistling cry of alarm.

Right: A ribbon of green at the valley bottom contrasts with the barren sandstone slopes above.

Far right: A newly hatched Robin Accentor in its nest, in a low bush at 5100 metres in Ladakh. This high-altitude breeder survives intense cold.

Centre right: Flowers of *Pedicularis longifolia* growing at 4000 metres.

Full moon over the Karakoram mountains.

Top: The brilliantly coloured Monal, or Impeyan Pheasant, of the Himalayas. Like all the other pheasant species, this bird has become rare due to extensive hunting and loss of habitat. Protected breeding reserves have now been established for them in India and Pakistan with the help of the Pheasant Trust and the World Wildlife Fund.

Above: The butterfly *Argymnis hyperbius*.

Left: The Central Asian Kingfisher, one of nearly 20 different species of kingfisher found in the Indian subcontinent.

Above: The delicately tinted water lily, *Nelumbo nucifera*, growing on the edges of the Nagin Lake in Kashmir, one of the many lakes which make this one of the most beautiful States of India. These lakes are important for wildlife, for elsewhere many lakes and marshes have been polluted or drained for land reclamation.

Above: The Hangul or Kashmir Stag, one of India's endangered deer species, is related to the European Red Deer. These are young males, but a fully-grown stag can weigh 180 kilograms and bear antlers with as many as 14 points. Their numbers have fallen from 5000 in 1930 to barely 500, and today their survival is threatened by competition for their only feeding area, in the most temperate part of Kashmir, from about 10,000 government-owned sheep.

Right: A wild Delphinium, *Delphinium himalayense*.

Top: Hangul hinds. These
stately deer can best be seen in the
Dachigam Reserve.

Above: A Holly Blue, or Hedge Blue Butterfly, one
of the *Lycaenopsina*.

Left: Himalayan Ibex, occurring at high altitudes from
Kashmir to Afghanistan in the Western Himalayas, are
noted for their massive, scimitar-shaped horns, which
can reach a length of more than one metre. (The record
is 147 centimetres.) They usually live in herds of 20 to
50, with a sentinel always alert. At the sound of its
whistling alarm, the herd dashes off at great speed,
rushing up or down steep cliffs with astonishing agility.

45

Top left and right: Both Brown Bear and Black Bear can be seen in the Dachigam Wildlife Sanctuary. The Himalayan Black Bear (left) is a very powerful animal, the males weighing up to 180 kilograms and sometimes growing up to two metres tall. Its glossy black fur, with a striking white 'V' across its chest, distinguishes it from the Brown Bear (right) and from the Sloth Bear (page 194) – which has a less distinctive 'V' on its shaggy fur. The Black Bear is found throughout the forested slopes of the Himalayas and eastward to Japan. It seldom ventures far above the tree line (3500 metres), but in winter descends into the Nepalese *terai* and Assam in search of food. It is a much more aggressive animal than the Brown Bear, which occurs within the Indian region only in the higher parts of the north-west Himalayas and in Ladakh. The Brown Bear avoids humans, but the Black Bear does not hesitate to attack wood-cutters or honey collectors if confronted. Both bears are very partial to the honey of wild bees.

Far left: The Indian Red Admiral butterfly *Vanessa indica*.

Far right: Wild raspberries – another favourite with the sweet-toothed bears.

Top left & right: Fungi of innumerable kinds play an important role in helping to break down the litter on the forest floor and return its nutrients to the soil. On the left is the toadstool *Coprinus disseminatus,* on the right the curious *Geastrum triplex.*

Above: Chukar Partridges in the Dachigam Sanctuary in Kashmir. They inhabit the drier regions of the Western Himalayas as far east as Central Nepal, at altitudes of 1200 – 5000 metres. Villagers often use them at festivals as substitutes for fighting cocks.

The Valley of Flowers in the Garhwal Himalaya of Uttar Pradesh is now well protected. This paradise for botanists has become a major tourist attraction, enabling people to see the fantastic floral profusion of the lower mountain slopes. High in the valley, the flowering shrub *Polygonum polystachya*, (in the foreground), is growing at an altitude of 3500 metres.

The famous Himalayan Blue Poppy
Meconopsis aculeata, which is now a favourite
garden plant in Europe. Yellow and scarlet
poppies also grow in the Himalayas.

The deep gorges in the Kedarnath
sanctuary provide some fine examples
of unexploited broad-leaved mixed
forests in the Himalayas.

Right: An ice bridge formed by a
waterfall in the Garhwal Himalayas.

Left and far left: The Musk Deer is one of the worst exploited animals of the Himalayas and the Tibetan highlands. Thousands are killed every year for the supposed value of the male's 'musk pods', which lie beneath the skin of its abdomen and produce the distinctive scent which functions as a sexual attraction. Both males and females are shot and netted indiscriminately. The pods are used as a basis for perfumes, and for medicinal purposes throughout Asia. (Japan represents the biggest market.) In effect, the pods are worth four times their weight in gold. Although the Musk Deer is now protected, this illicit 'merchandise' is still smuggled by way of the high passes from Tibet through Nepal to the Indian or Burmese ports. These inoffensive little creatures (they stand only 50 cm at the shoulder) live in the birch thickets above the conifers. Their large, splayed hooves provide a secure grip on the icy slopes. In the absence of horns, their long, projecting canine teeth are used for defence. During the day they lie hidden in snow hollows, coming out at dusk to feed. Unlike most deer, they live singly or in pairs. Lacking the protection of a herd, they are very vulnerable to predators as well as human hunters.

Above: The brilliant flower of *Potentilla nepalensis*.

Left: Near the headwaters of the Ganges is the sacred Hemkund glacial lake, to which thousands of Sikhs from all over India make an arduous pilgrimage on foot during the summer months (June-October). During the rest of the year, the snows make the lake inaccessible.

Overleaf: One of the most colourful flowers to be seen in the Valley of Flowers – a mass of *Impatiens sulcata*.

Mount Annapurna (8078 metres) in late afternoon sunlight.

The expanded hood of the Spectacled Cobra (far left), identified by the characteristic mark on the back of the hood, and the sheathed flower of the Snake Lily, *Arisaema nepanthoides* (left), display a striking resemblance. Three kinds of cobra occur in India: the Spectacled Cobra, the Monocled Cobra and the Black Cobra. The much larger King Cobra, or Hamadryad, is a different species and restricted to the tropical eastern rain-forests. Although the cobra's venomous bite can be fatal to humans, these snakes play an important role in helping to control the vast population of rats and other rodents which annually consume thousands of tons of India's stored grain. In some parts of the country shrines are erected for the worship of cobras, which are pulled out of their holes and venerated in the villages – apparently without the handlers being bitten. They are then gently returned, unharmed, to their hiding places.

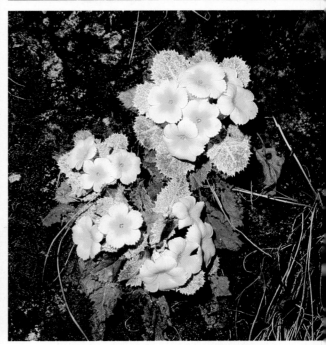

Top right: Primulas of many colours, such as the pink *Primula gracilipes* (above) and the yellow *Primula auriata* (below) brighten the upper slopes.

Right: Orchids in great profusion also grow in the lower forests; the beautiful *Dendrobium aphyllum* is a typical example.

Far left: The great forests of Himalayan Hemlock, *Tsuga dumosa*, and various firs and pines which once covered the lower slopes of the Nepalese Himalayas are rapidly disappearing because of the country's dependence on wood for fuel and building.

Top and above left: No flowers of the Himalayas can be more spectacular, nor grow in greater variety and profusion, than the rhododendron. The scarlet *Rhododendron arboreum* is one of several species that grow to a height of 20 metres.
Above right: At high altitudes, the scarlet Rhododendron is replaced by a pink variety of the same species, *R.a. cinnamomeum*.

Right: The Red Panda lives in the bamboo thickets of Sikkim's temperate forests. Its bright reddish-orange fur and white face are conspicuous in daylight, but this animal usually spends most of the day sleeping, curled up on a high tree branch.

Above: The 'Slipper' orchid: *Paphiopedilum spicerianum*.

Top left and bottom right: The Red Lacewing butterfly *Cethosia biblis* with wings open and closed.

Top right: A yellow orchid: *Cymbidium elegans*.

Above: Mount Kanchengjunga from the mountain-top town of Darjeeling. Rising to 8197 metres, it guards the frontier between Sikkim and Tibet, where its peaks are called 'The Five Treasures of Eternal Snows'. Such views are possible only in the clear conditions that follow the months of the monsoon.

Right: A female Muntjak, or Barking Deer. Its name is derived from its distinctive dog-like barking call. It is fairly numerous in the thickly wooded hills up to an altitude of about 2500 metres, and is one of the favourite prey species of Tigers and Leopards. The males have short, two-pronged antlers.

Left: The Teesta River winds through the forested mountains of Sikkim. A rough road follows most of its course and provides access to some impressive scenery on the way to the capital, Gangtok.

Below: None of the small cats of India is more handsome than the fierce little Leopard Cat, which occurs in forests throughout the country. It has been much persecuted for its beautiful fur, but is now protected by law.

Above: The Hill Fox is the most likely of the three distinct races of the Red Fox to be seen in the Himalayan region. Like all foxes, it is a self-reliant and rather solitary animal, and eats a wide variety of food ranging from berries and offal to small birds and rodents. It is common around hill villages but seldom seen in the forest. The Indian Fox lives in the lowland plains.

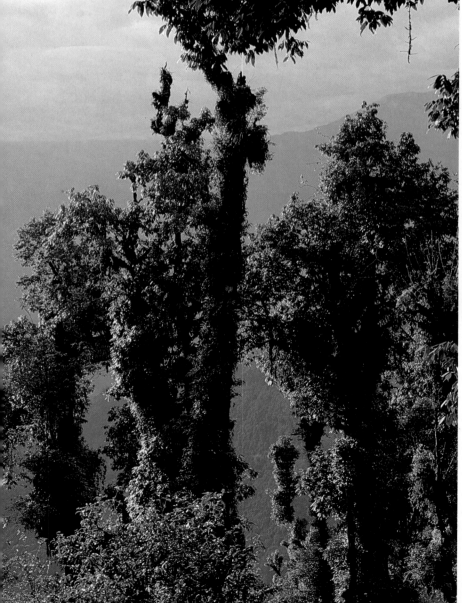

Left: Oaks festooned with mosses and epiphytic orchids in Sikkim's Mainam Forest Reserve.

Left: Forests are being destroyed for fuel or building throughout the Himalayan foothills, and scenes of devastation are commonplace. The top-soil in felled areas is soon washed away by the monsoon rains, exposing villages to severe flooding.

Below left: The delicate flowers of the orchid *Pleione praecox* growing on a fallen oak in the Mainam reserve.

Below right: The Goral is a goat-antelope of which two types, the grey and the brown, occur in the Himalayas at altitudes of 700 to 4000 metres. They have short, backward-curving horns and a distinctive, hissing alarm-cry.

Far left: The curious acorns of the evergreen oak *Lithocarpus pachyphylla* in the Mainam Wildlife Reserve.

Centre left: Larvae of a Lymantriid moth in a communal nest.

Left: The Himalayan Palm Civet is distinguished from the various other civets of India by the absence of stripes or spots on its body, and by its long white whiskers. All the civets are useful as voracious hunters of rats, although this species feeds chiefly on fruit.

Overleaf: The peak of Mt. Kabur seen from Western Sikkim.

65

The Indo-Gangetic Plain
The Heartland of India

The great Indo-Gangetic Plain, forming the foredrop of the Himalayas, is probably the largest area of deposited alluvial soil in the world. No borehole has ever reached its base, thought to lie as deep as 13,000 metres. It consists of muds and sands washed down over the millennia from the Himalayan watershed, and even far below sea level it is still fine-grained. The seasonal rain-bearing winds of the monsoon, which sweep back and forth across the plain, make it one of the most productive, as well as one of the most densely populated regions on earth.

Its seemingly inexhaustible richness has tempted countless foreign invaders from less hospitable lands who laid waste so many of India's cities before being either repelled or quietly absorbed. This is the heartland of India and the chief source of its nourishment.

Three distinct river systems water the great plain. One rises from the western Himalayas as the Indus and its tributaries, reaching the Arabian Sea near Karachi in Pakistan. The second, which also rises in this region, turns immediately eastwards among the mountains, past Lhasa in Tibet, finally to flow southward through eastern Assam as the Brahmaputra. The third has many tributaries, all draining the southern slopes of the Himalayas and uniting to form the mighty Ganges, the holy river of India.

To the north of the plain, at the foot of the Himalayas, malaria once prevented development of the lowland *terai*, but with the virtual eradication of the disease the region has been rapidly exploited. The hill farmers have swarmed down to cultivate the rich alluvial soil. The emerald green of paddyfields is now marching steadily forward and domestic cattle are replacing much of the wildlife for which the *terai* was once famous. Fortunately, HM King Mahendra and his successor HM King Birendra acted in time to save Nepal's Tigers, One-horned Rhinoceroses and Barasingha Deer by creating the Royal Chitwan National Park and the Karnali and Sukla Phanta Wildlife Reserves. Here substantial areas of the beautiful forests and grassy swamps of the *terai* are expertly managed and protected for the benefit of wildlife and the future generations of Nepalis.

To the far west lies the hot and arid region of the Indus plain, embracing Punjab, Sind, Rajasthan, Kutch and northern Gujarat. Even these areas were not always desert. Archaeological finds have revealed that there was once a flourishing civilization here in the Indus valley. Poor agricultural practices, deforestation and overgrazing eventually turned the region into an arid plain where water-dependent wildlife could not survive. Deforestation and desertification has continued on the desert fringe, and it has been estimated that the desert is extending in the north-west at the rate of roughly eight kilometres every decade. Yet even the desert has attractions for the naturalist in its specially adapted vegetation and desert animals such as the famous Wild Asses of the Thar desert in the southwest, which live on the immense salt flats of the Little Rann of Kutch, or the large, and beautiful, but much endangered, Great Indian Bustards of Rajasthan.

To the east, benefitting from very high monsoon rainfall, lie the lush tropical, semi-evergreen forests of Assam, the Bangladesh Hill Tracts and the tribal areas of Burma. Both the Brahmaputra and the Ganges make their tortuous way to the Bay of Bengal through the labyrinth of the Sundarbans swamps. The name Sundarbans means 'beautiful forest', and it is indeed a region of exceptional biotic richness. This is the largest mangrove forest in the world. The mean temperature here exceeds 28°C (80°F), reaching 43°C (109°F) in March. The annual rainfall is about 3.5 metres. The viscous, muddy ground into which one can sink above the knees is created entirely by river-borne silt trapped by the mangrove roots. These arch out from the trees into the mud, where regiments of bayonet-like spikes, the pneumatophore roots, are exposed at low tide to obtain the oxygen which the saline mud cannot provide.

One third of the Sundarbans is in India and heavily populated (except for a large Tiger Reserve), but there are relatively few humans in the Bangladesh two-thirds: only fishermen in their picturesque boats and honey-collectors and woodcutters in their canoes, who ply from Khulna down the long labyrinth of muddy channels. Tigers here are completely aquatic, swimming strongly from island to island. During my explorations I found their pug marks on an island 4.5 kilometres out in the Bay of Bengal. From the vantage point of a boat one can see Chital Deer, Wild Pigs, Estuarine Crocodiles, Macaque Monkeys and several hundred species of birds. Even the shining mud along the creeks is full of life: bug-eyed little amphibian Mud Skippers row themselves up the banks on their dorsal fins, and colourful Fiddler Crabs urgently pirouette and wave their grotesquely big single claws like semaphores to attract females to their holes. There are some areas of mangrove on the west coast of India and at the mouth of the Indus in Pakistan, but nowhere in such magnificence or extent as in the 80,000 square kilometres of the Sundarbans delta.

The central plain is vast. Cities and tens of thousands of small villages are scattered across it, but lost in its huge scale. Here, 15 per cent of the world's population toil on the land. The great majority are poor, living patiently from one season to the next, trusting that the harvest will not fail and leave them destitute. Many are too poor to own a plot of land; they follow a nomadic share-cropping existence, moving from one district to another, to weed, or harvest, or plant at the behest of the rich landowners.

Most of the natural vegetation of the plain has been severly damaged by the constant search for fuel, which can be provided only by lopping or felling the fast disappearing trees, or by burning dried cow-dung. Nevertheless, in this region are some of India's most renowned and valuable National Parks and Wildlife Reserves, which a far-sighted Government has succeeded in protecting from the human pressures beyond their boundaries. In such carefully preserved areas as Kanha, Corbett, Kaziranga and many others can still be seen the full magnificence of India's original vegetation and wildlife. Nowhere can a more beautiful tract of open Sal forest be seen than in the Kanha Tiger Reserve. When one of its now numerous Tigers stalks majestically in daylight through the trees, the sight is unforgettable. Few places can compare with the splendour of Corbett National Park, set against the backdrop of the lovely Siwalik Hills, where wild Elephants still roam. To ride a well-trained Elephant through the marshes of Kaziranga National Park, among its many One-horned Rhinoceroses, wild Buffaloes and countless deer is a privilege beyond words.

The Clouded Leopard has abnormally long canines.

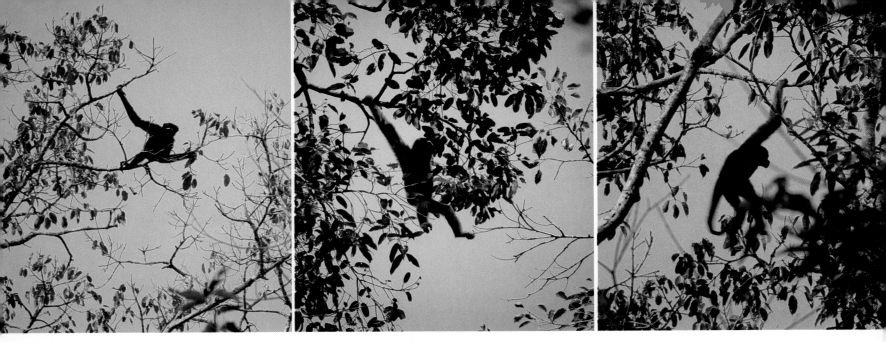

The Hoolock Gibbon is the only true ape found in India. It occurs in the hill forests of Assam and in the Bangladesh Hill Tracts, where it swings from tree to tree with amazing agility. This gibbon's extremely long arms and lack of a tail make its appearance unmistakable. The male is black, with conspicuous white eyebrows, while the female is pale brown. Gibbons advertise their presence long before they can be seen with astonishingly loud *whoop-whoop* cries which can be heard for nearly a kilometre. Next to the deep-throated roar of a tiger, the duetted chorus of gibbons is probably the most romantic and thrilling sound to be heard anywhere. When a gibbon is calling, it inflates its throat like a balloon to produce a great volume of sound (second from right).

Above: A Buffalo cow guarding her twin calves among burned elephant grass, where they feed on the succulent young shoots.

A Pallas's Fishing Eagle in the Kaziranga National Park.

Left: Wild Buffaloes before a stand of elephant grass in Kaziranga National Park, in Assam, where there are still considerable numbers. Their massive horns, triangular in section, can have a span of more than two metres. Whereas domestic buffaloes are the epitome of docility, being led or ridden by children in the paddy fields, their wild relatives are extremely shy of humans and difficult to approach. They can be very aggressive, the bulls sometimes killing domestic bulls that show an interest in their cows. They have even been known to attack tigers which prey on the cows and calves, though they rarely succeed in driving them away.

After the Elephant, the One-horned Rhinoceros is the largest animal in the subcontinent. The biggest surviving population is in the Kaziranga National Park in Assam, where they can be approached quite closely by tourists riding well-trained elephants. Although the rhinos appear to be very tame, it is inadvisable to approach a cow with calf: the park wardens often have to fire a shot in the air in order to avoid being charged. Poachers everywhere kill rhinos for the high sums fetched by their horns, which are believed to have magical or medicinal properties.

Below: The Lesser Adjutant Stork is a useful scavenger with a fondness for carrion.

Right: Elephants feeding in the marsh beside a *jheel*.

Above: A few wild Elephants can be seen in the Kaziranga National Park, where they feed in the cane-brakes or bathe in the marshes. Although there are still fairly large numbers left in India, the population is steadily declining because of the constant reduction of undisturbed forests on which they depend. Unlike African Elephants, they avoid open country unless driven by hunger to seek food in cultivated areas, where they severely damage crops. The breaking up of the great forests has resulted in serious interference with their seasonal migrations, and has led to increased conflict with farmers. Special measures are now being taken in India, Bhutan and Bangladesh to provide protected areas large enough for these splendid animals.

Left: A Crested Serpent Eagle
with a snake it has just caught.

Below: A group of Spot-billed Pelicans perch in a flowering Silk-cotton.

Left: Male and female (far left) Hog Deer grazing in burned elephant grass in the Kaziranga National Park. The name is derived from their habit of scuttling through the undergrowth with their heads held low, like wild pigs. Although Tigers and Leopards find them easy prey, they remain plentiful in northern India.

Above: Herds of Barasingha, or Swamp Deer, graze in the extensive marshes of the Kaziranga National Park. This group is made up only of hinds or young, the stags living in bachelor herds outside the rutting season. There are three races of Barasingha, and these are identified by the shape of their hooves. Those in the the Kaziranga in Assam belong to the *ranjitsinhi* race, which have large, splayed hooves suited to soft ground. Further west in the Dudhwa National Park in Uttar Pradesh State and in Nepal, is the slightly different *duvauceli* race and in the Kanha National Park in Madhya Pradesh is the *branderi* race, which has neat, small hooves well suited to the hard ground of that region.

Overleaf: A frosty morning in a forested valley in Meghalaya, between Shillong and Cherrapunji. The trees are *Pinus khasya*.

Right: The Thamin, or Brow-antlered Deer is a severely endangered species, now restricted in India to the 'phumdi', quaking swamps, of Keibul Lamjao National Park in Manipur. This stag is following a hind across the boggy ground. Even this habitat is today gravely imperilled by outside pressures.

Below: The coarse dark coat and long brow-tines are typical of the male Thamin. These deer live in small herds, hiding by day and emerging to feed at dusk and in the early morning.

Above: The semi-aquatic habitat of the Thamin is best approached by boat along a channel cut through the swamp.

Right: White-winged Wood Ducks are now extremely rare, but a few still exist in sheltered pools in the evergreen rain-forests of Assam and in the Chittagong Hill Tracts. Special reserves have been created for them, and the stocks have been supplemented with birds raised by the Wildfowl Trust in England.

Left: A Thamin fawn.

Left: The shy Serow is a goat-antelope which lives in the rocky, wooded gorges of the Himalayas and in the Mishmi Hills in Assam. Its short, cylindrical horns grow from pedicles just above the eyes.

81

Below left: Sheer cliffs with waterfalls are typical of the rugged scenery of the Cherrapunji escarpment near Shillong. The deep forested gorges (below right) provide secure refuge for many forms of wildlife.

Above: The Slow Loris belongs to the Lemur family, and is found in the forests of North-east India and in the Hill Tracts of Bangladesh. This gentle, slow-moving little creature – only 35 cm long – feeds mainly on insects. It sometimes feeds upside-down, hanging by its hind feet and holding food in its hands. The Slow Loris also drinks upside-down from water trapped in the hollow of a branch. It is often seen as a pet in villages.

Left & far left: The elusive Binturong, often called the Bear Cat, belongs to the Civet family. It has dense, grizzled fur and long white whiskers, and spends most of its time in the trees, climbing rather slowly with the aid of its long, bushy, prehensile tail. Like all the civets, it is omnivorous, feeding chiefly on fruit, small birds and insects. Its range is from Nepal and Assam eastwards into Burma and peninsular Malaya.

Among India's many species of monkeys, none is more beautiful than the Golden Langur, shown here in the Bhutan Manas Reserve. It was first discovered near the Sankosh River by the naturalist tea-planter, E. P. Gee, in 1953. With its silky, pale gold fur and exceptionally long tail, it never fails to evoke exclamations of admiration from anyone fortunate enough to see one.

Above: An Elephant in the Manas Forest takes a dust bath, a habit in which elephants delight in the absence of water. The Indian species is easily distinguished from the African elephant by its smaller ears and more rounded back. Unlike the African elephant, it is an animal of the dense forests – where there are plenty of bamboo thickets in which to shelter. It also occurs in humid jungles and in hilly or even mountainous regions, emerging at dusk to feed in the valleys. In Sikkim it has even been recorded above the snow line at 3660 metres. The cows have only rudimentary tusks, while those of the bulls rarely match the length of the African species.

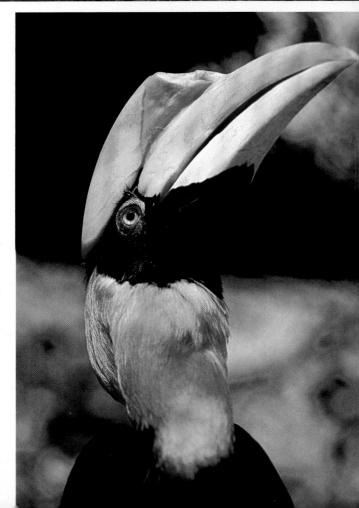

Right: The Great Indian Hornbill is the largest of the half-dozen Indian species. It is easily distinguished by its huge bill (with a yellow casque) and its broad black and white wings, which make a distinctive noise – like those of a Mute Swan – in flight. Like all the hornbills, it is now suffering from the loss of old forest trees, with large cavities in which to nest.

Ábove: An Elephant in the Manas Forest.

Centre left: The fallen flower of a Silk Cotton Tree, *Bombax ceiba*.

Left: A Hoary-bellied Himalayan Squirrel in the hill forests of Manas.

Above and top: The large and handsome Malayan Giant Squirrel can be seen in Nepal, Bhutan and Assam. It is recognized by its almost black upper parts and bright orange-buff underparts. When alarmed by a predator, such as a Leopard, it gives a very loud, rattling cry which can be heard for a great distance.

Left: The broad Manas River divides India from the Kingdom of Bhutan. By good co-operative planning, the Indian and Bhutan Manas Reserves now adjoin on either side of the river, providing one of the largest protected areas for wildlife in the subcontinent. The reserves also form one of the least despoiled areas of continuous primary forest, and are exceptionally rich in rare species of animals and plants. Animal photography in such dense forest is difficult, partly because the ground is usually carpeted with dry fallen leaves which crackle underfoot and alarm the animals.

Left: The delicate white flowers of a species of *Apolynaceae*.

Below left: The Muntjak or Barking Deer, whose dog-like barking call is easily imitated. Manas Forest.

Below: The Capped Langur of Assam.

Above and right: The large Water Monitor is one of the many strange amphibious creatures that live in the Sundarbans. It prowls the labyrinth of muddy channels, digging up the eggs of turtles and crocodiles and killing rodents and nesting birds.

Left: The largest area of mangrove swamp in the world is in the Sundarbans, at the mouth of the Ganges and Brahmaputra rivers. The dominant tree species is the Sundri, *Heritiera minor*, with dense clumps of various palms such as *Phoenix paludosa* (foreground) – favourite tiger habitat. A third of the Sundarbans lies in India, with the remaining two-thirds in Bangladesh.

Below right: To land here is to sink up to the thighs in the glutinous mud and to stumble among the intricately interwoven arched roots of the mangroves. These roots trap the silt from the water and gradually build up islands. To obtain oxygen, which the saline mud cannot provide, the trees grow regiments of bayonet-like spikes from their roots, which at low tide are exposed to the air.

Above: Everywhere are thousands of colourful Fiddler Crabs, named after their habit of waving a grotesquely large claw to attract females to their holes.

Centre top: The bug-eyed little Mud Skipper is an amphibious fish which 'rows' itself up the banks on its dorsal fins to feed among the mangrove roots.

Right: At Bhittar Kanika Reserve, on the Orissa coast, salt-water Estuarine Crocodiles can be seen basking on the banks of the Mahanadi River. At one time they were very nearly exterminated by skin traders, but here and elsewhere there are now special breeding and research centres where they are beginning to recover.

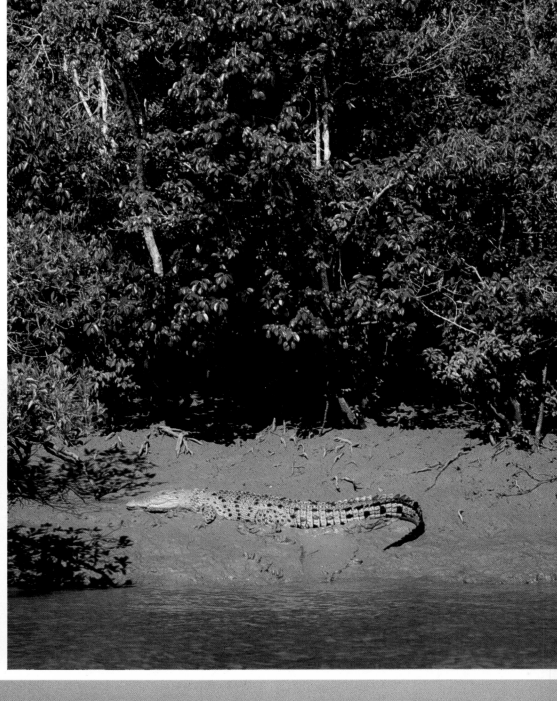

Below: A handsome Black Carpenter Bee, *Xylocopa sp.*, feeding on a *Crotolaria* flower.

Bottom: *Borassus* and *Phoenix* palms against the sunset.

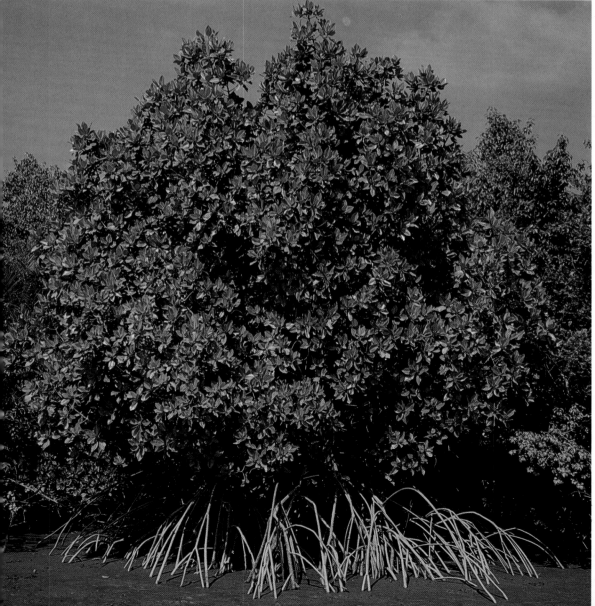

Above: The Pangolin, or Scaly Anteater, is a familiar animal throughout India. It feeds on termites or ants, which are dug out with powerful claws. During daylight, the Pangolin is usually hidden in a deep burrow, coming out to feed in the evenings. A ponderous walker, this animal supports most of its weight on very long, in-turned front claws. When surprised, it rolls itself up into an impregnable ball.

Left: There are about 20 species of mangroves in the Sundarbans and along the Orissa coast, the most typical being those with long arched roots, like the *Bruguiera gymnorhiza* shown here.

Left: Long-billed Vultures are common in India. They roam the skies at very high altitudes, looking for carrion and watching each other. The moment one bird drops, the others immediately follow it down to the carcass, so that scores may assemble in a matter of minutes.

Below: A Blue Tiger Butterfly, *Tirumala limniace* – one of the milkweed group.

Bottom: The Chilka Lake bird sanctuary in Orissa.

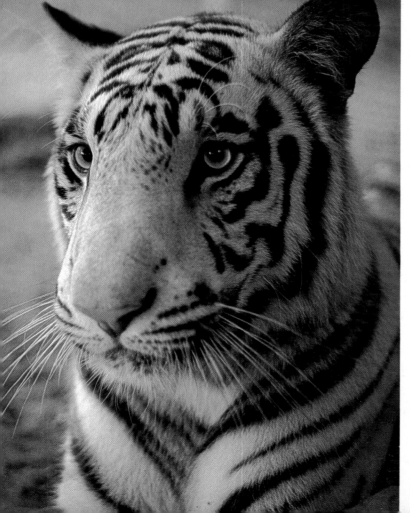

Above and left: The White Tigers of Rewa are world famous. They are neither albinos (which would have pink eyes) nor a separate species, but are what scientists call 'recessive mutants'. In 1951 a white cub was trapped in the Rewa forest and kept as a pet by the local Maharajah, who mated it to a normal captive tigress. She produced three normal litters. One of her cubs was later mated with the white sire, producing a litter of white cubs which were the ancestors of others now in many zoos.

Overleaf: A Tiger in Kanha National Park. The Tiger is India's magnificent 'national animal' and was the subject of India's most famous conservation effort.

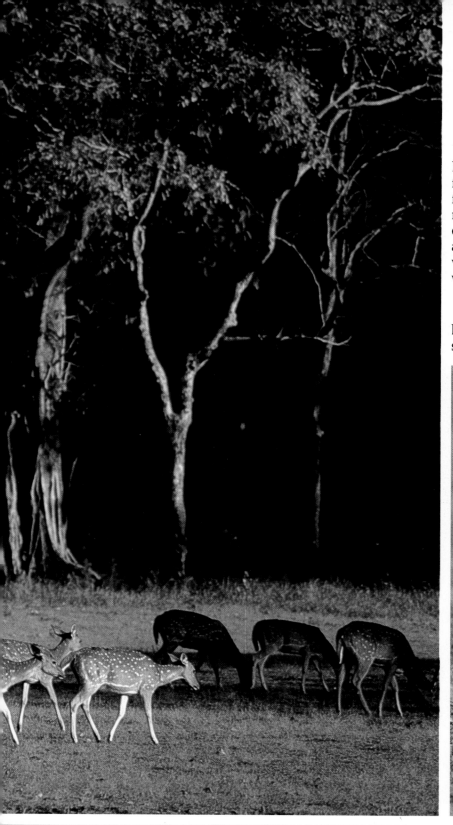

Left and bottom: The Kanha National Park in Madhya Pradesh is noted for its open Sal forests, which the Chital, or Spotted Deer, particularly favours. It is generally regarded as the most beautiful of the world's many deer species, and is now common in the forest glades of many of India's wildlife reserves. The stag's antlers have only three long tines, and their coats are sometimes almost black. The antlers are dropped at varying times in different localities, although pairing is usually in the winter. Fawns may be seen in all seasons.

Below: A Little Green Bee-eater, one of a number of colourful species of this family in India.

Above left: A mixed flock of Green Pigeons, Blossom-headed Parakeets and Rose-ringed Parakeets.

Far left: Dholes, or Wild Dogs, in the Kanha National Park. They hunt in packs with ruthless efficiency, preying mainly on deer. Occasionally they pull down young tigers.

Left: Jackals scavenge around all villages, but are now much less numerous than they used to be.

Above: Although Gaur Jungle Bison look so powerful (a bull weighs nearly one ton), they are timid and retiring creatures. Family groups spend most of the day hidden in the dense hill forests, descending to the grassy valleys to feed at dusk and dawn. Once fairly widely distributed in the hilly regions, it is now very localised. Gaur can be seen in such wildlife reserves as Chitwan in Nepal and Bandipur and Mudumalai in southern India, as well as at Kanha.

Above, top and right: There are some fine herds of the *branderi* race of Barasingha in the Kanha National Park, where they are a favoured prey species of Tigers. The stags have dark coats and well-branched antlers. When fully grown, they can weigh up to 180 kg, with heavy manes and antlers measuring up to 75 cm. Barasingha are strongly gregarious. If alarmed, they will dash off with a loud chorus of distinctive baying. The Kanha population is now approaching 500. It is gratifying to note that the Baiga and Gond tribal people of the region, who used to be skilled hunters of the Swamp Deer, now take obvious pride in protecting the wildlife in this superb reserve.

Below left: Mynah birds feed off parasites on a
Barasingha hind.

Below right: The colourful Indian Roller is common
throughout the country.

The Bandhogarh National Park in Madhya Pradesh State has a wide range of wildlife species, including Tigers and some rare birds. It is a scenically remarkable area, with high rocky outcrops and cliffs.

Right: A pair of Black Ibises.

Below: A Dusky Horned Owl, with its 'horns' depressed.

Below right: This rocky cliff is typical of the Park's terrain, which is crowned with an ancient fortress and temple ruins.

Above: The Crested Serpent Eagle is fairly common in the wooded parts of the northern half of India. It is replaced to the south of the Gangetic Plain by a slightly smaller race, the Lesser Crested Eagle. As its name implies, it feeds on snakes, lizards and frogs, but also takes crabs, eels and small birds. It often soars to a great height, when it is readily identified by its distinctive high whistling cry.

Left: When suspicious, and during courtship, the Crested Serpent Eagle erects its fan-shaped crest.

In 1940 there were perhaps 40,000 Tigers in India. By 1969 a census showed that only 1826 survived. Excessive hunting and loss of forest habitat had caused this catastrophic decline, and it was clear that unless an enormous effort could be made to save them, Tigers would be extinct within 20 years. With the help of a world-wide campaign organized by the World Wildlife Fund, the Indian Government launched 'Project Tiger'. This resulted in a complete ban on hunting and the creation of 15 fully protected Tiger reserves. Thanks to skillful management of the vegetation and water sources, not only Tigers and their prey species, but all wildlife has benefited. The Tiger population has more than doubled and the species is saved for posterity.

Above and right: Tiger cubs with their mother.

Top right: A tree regularly used by a Tiger for sharpening its claws.

The Chitwan National Park is expertly managed, and has been the scene of a number of important wildlife research projects in which Nepalese, British and American scientists have shared the work. The first studies of the territorial behaviour of Tigers by means of radio telemetry were conducted there, the tigers being fitted with collars bearing miniature radio transmitters. This research was under the auspices of the Nepalese Government, the Smithsonian Institution and the World Wildlife Fund, and today there is still close co-operation between Nepalese and Indian tiger experts. Tourists from the 'Tiger Tops Lodge' can watch One-horned Rhinoceroses and Sloth Bears and several species of deer feeding in the marshes. There are also well-hidden hides from which Tigers and Leopards can be seen at night. In the rivers there are both Mugger Crocodiles and Gharials as well as Gangetic Dolphins. More than 350 species of birds have been recorded in the Park.

Right: The banks of the Rapti River in the Royal Chitwan National Park in Nepal provide an admirable vantage point for the panorama of changing colours on the distant Himalayas, photographed late on a November day. The snowy peaks are over 200 km away, and such views are possible only in the clear air that follows the monsoon.

Top left: There are many marshy pools and streams in the Chitwan National Park where Tigers bathe and Rhinoceroses wallow.

Above: A male Iora at its nest, woven of fine grasses and spiders' webs.

Right: A parasitic 'left-handed' Strangler Fig squeezing the life out of the host tree in its struggle to reach the sunlight.

Opposite: The presence of Rhinoceroses is easily detected by the big heaps of dung with which they mark their territories and to which they repeatedly return, backing up to the heap to add a new quota. The habit is well-known to poachers, who dig camouflaged pit traps along the established approach tracks. Strangely enough, a few old rhinos lose their aggressive spirit and stay near villages, even allowing children to ride on them. However, such behaviour is exceptional.

Below: The Green Pit Viper occurs in the Nepalese *terai*. Like the Cobra and other venomous species, it helps to control the huge rat population.

Bottom left: The butterfly, *Papilio polytes*.

Bottom right: The so-called 'bloodsucker' or Garden Lizard, *Calotes versicolor*.

Right: The Chitwan reserve affords an opportunity to see fully adult Gharials; a breeding project for them has been established on the Rapti River in the Park. Males can grow up to 7 metres long, and have large, bulbous tips to their upper jaws. In spite of their size and fierce appearance, they are harmless fish-eaters. Those shown below are only two years old.

Right and below: The Dudhwa National Park, on the
border between India and Nepal, is one of the strongholds
of the Barasingha Swamp Deer, with a particularly fine
herd of 2600 of the *duvauceli* race. It is also the home of a
considerable number of Tigers and Leopards. It was here
that the famous naturalist, Billy Arjan Singh, reared
several orphaned tiger and leopard cubs and successfully
returned them to the wild, a feat never achieved before.
He was largely instrumental in the creation of the park,
which has some tracts of very beautiful forest and
extensive grassy *maidans* where the deer feed.

115

Below: The Red Jungle Fowl, the progenitor of the domestic chicken.

Left and centre: Peafowl are numerous in the Dudhwa reserve. The magnificent fan is displayed during the male's courtship dance, which occurs during the later part of the dry season.

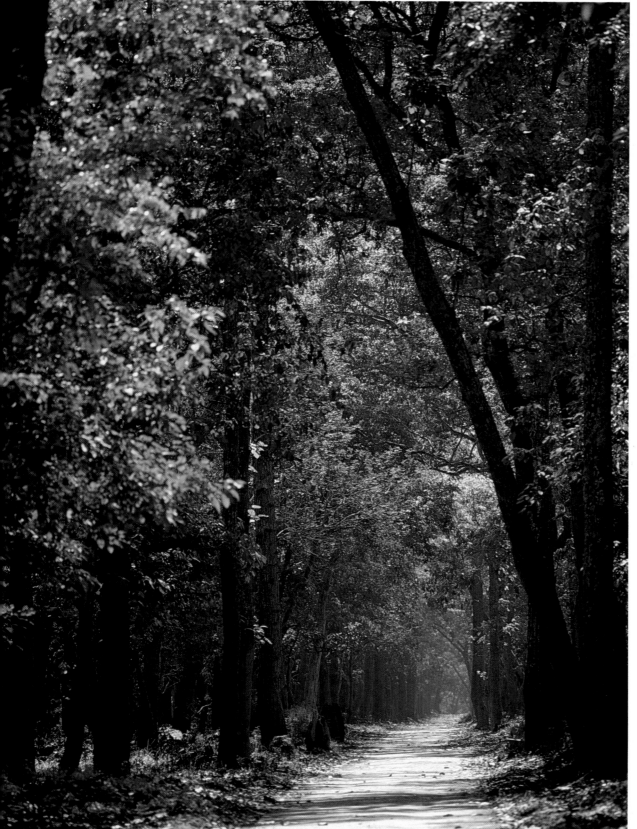

Far left: A walk in the Dudhwa at dawn reveals the full beauty of the forest as the sun illuminates its rich colours.

Left: The red tree along this forest path is a Kusim, or *Schleichera oleosa*. The bright colour is provided by the tree's young leaves.

117

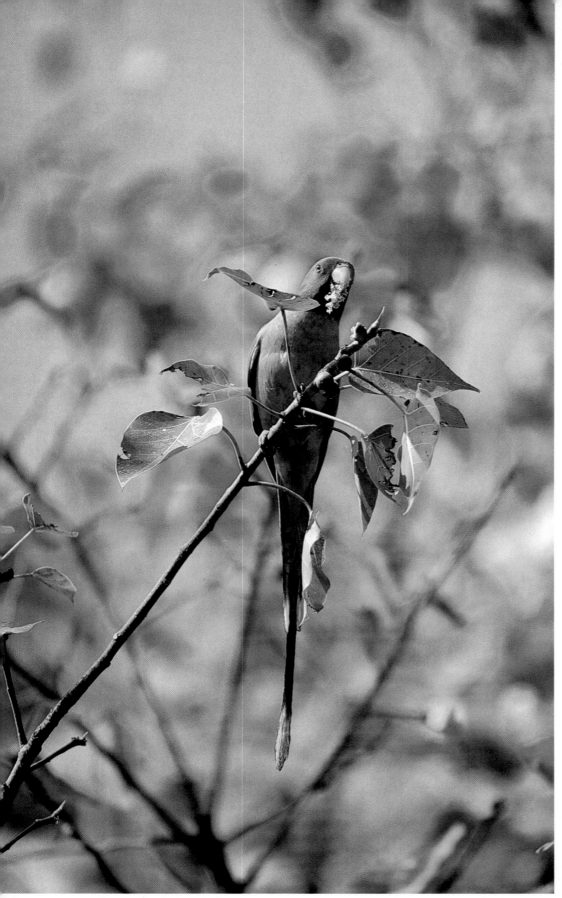

Far left: The Corbett National Park at dawn. The Park, in Uttar Pradesh, was named after the renowned hunter-naturalist, Jim Corbett, who was the first to publicize the threats to the survival of the Tiger in the 1940s. The park is scenically magnificent, set against the backdrop of the Siwalik Hills, with the Ramganga River winding through it. The recent damming of the river just downstream of this point deprived the wild elephants of their favourite feeding area and interrupted their long established seasonal route. However, the park remains one of the most attractive in India, and is still rich in wildlife.

Left: A Blossom-headed Parakeet eating a wild fig.

Below left: A White-breasted Kingfisher.

Below: A Long-tailed Nightjar in the Corbett National Park.

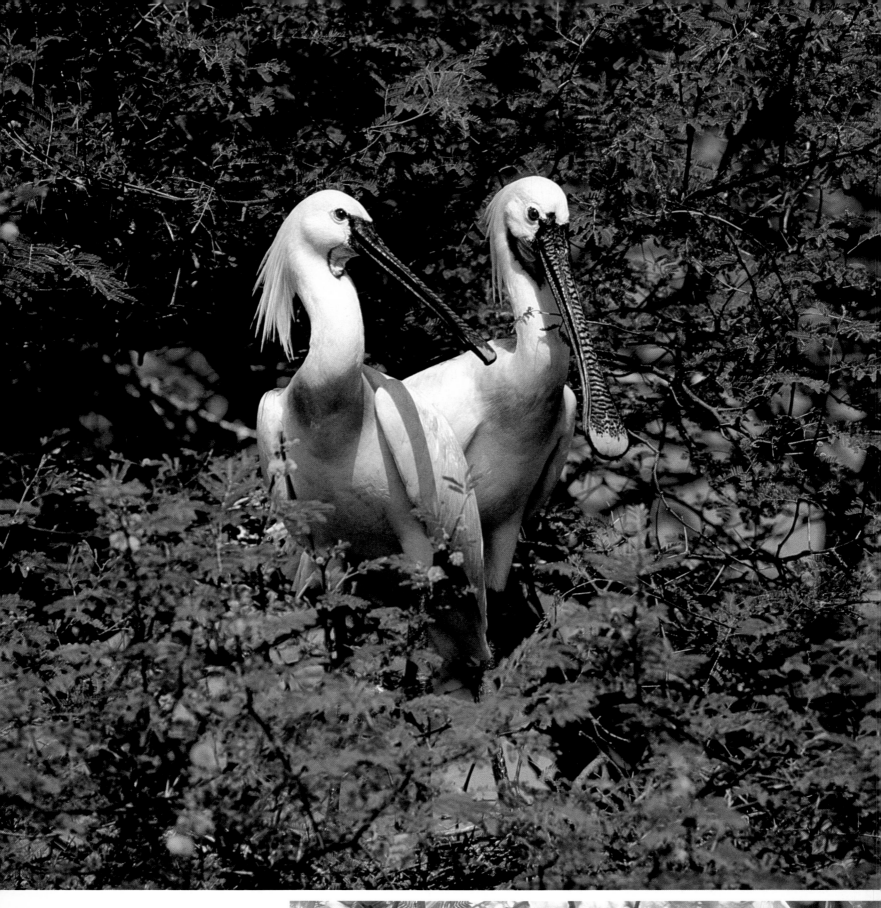

Right: A pair of the attractive little Collared Scops Owls, whose quiet *'wheet . . . wheet'* cry can be monotonous at night. The Indian sub-continent has nearly 50 different species and regional sub-species of owl.

Far left: Spoonbills can be seen in many wetland areas in India, Nepal and Bangladesh. In breeding plumage, with long, drooping crests and bright orange feathers at the base of the neck, they are very handsome birds. Part of the Indian population is migratory. Spoonbills breed in mixed colonies, with various storks, ibises and herons as close neighbours.

Left and below: A Spoonbill carries a large twig to add to its nest.

Above and right: A courtship ritual of
the Rose-ringed Parakeet. This bright green
species is common in all city parks and
gardens, its noisy flocks dashing around the
roof-tops. Although handsome, it can
ravage cereal and fruit crops. Marauding
flocks ignore the slings and catapults of the
bird-scarers posted on their *machans* around
the fields. These birds nest under roof-tiles
and in cavities in wayside trees, not only in
towns, but also in forested and even arid
regions. These pictures show a courting pair.
Courtships involve mutual preening, the
passing of food to the female and a curious
clawing of the air by the male followed
by wild chases in flight.

Below: Pintail Ducks in Bharatpur Bird Sanctuary.

Below centre: Red-crested Pochard feeding.

Bottom: A Five-striped Ground Squirrel.

Above: White Ibises, of which hundreds nest
in congested colonies.

The bird sanctuary at Bharatpur, now part of the Keoladeo
Ghana National Park in Rajasthan, provides one of the
greatest wildlife spectacles in India. Its many ponds, tree-
lined *bunds* and lush meadows are literally crowded with a
vast congregation of birds of many kinds. It is also an
important centre for bird-ringing and ornithological research,
much of which is organized by the Bombay Natural History
Society, and for public education by the Indian branch of
the World Wildlife Fund.

Right: White Ibis chicks can barely move
in their overcrowded nest.

Left: A White-backed Vulture with chick
at its huge nest.

Right: Painted Storks also
nest by the hundred in the
Bharatpur Reserve.

Above: The most important visitors to Bharatpur are the ultra-rare
Siberian Cranes, a pair of which is shown here. Every year a flock
arrives from the USSR to winter in the safety of the reserve. Their
number has steadily declined, however, and the world population
may now be fewer than 40 birds. Ornithologists gather every year
to watch their fascinating courtship 'dancing'.

Right: A Nilgai cow and Cattle Egret in the Bharatpur marshes.

Left: Young Intermediate Egrets at their nest.

Below: A Darter drying its wings after swimming beneath the water in one of the ponds.

Bottom: Even at dusk and before sunrise, the ponds are alive with birds.

Right: The Openbill Stork is the most numerous of India's various storks. Its curiously shaped bill is specially adapted to slicing open the shells of the snails and other crustaceans on which it feeds. The Openbill Stork has a remarkable display flight, descending vertically, twisting and turning while 'pedalling' its long legs vigorously.

Below: A huge flight of Greylag geese take off from the Bharatpur marshes.

Left: An Open-billed Stork.

Above: A Black-necked Stork. This handsome but rather solitary bird with coral-red legs has the black areas of its plumage glossed with purple, blue and bronze, making it one of the most attractive of the storks.

Left: The Tawny Eagle is a common species throughout India. It is rather lethargic, feeding mainly on carrion or forcing other raptors to relinquish their prey.

Far left and below left: Birds are so numerous at Bharatpur that there is a shortage of nesting sites. Colonial species such as Painted Storks nest so closely together in the acacias that their nests merge, leading to continuous squabbling and much stealing of twigs.

Left: A Painted Stork in flight.

Below: Often a single tree houses several different species. Two pairs of Spoonbills have built nests directly beneath those in which young Painted Storks are standing. A Grey Heron and a Darter fish from the same tree.

Right: The Nilgai, or Blue Bull, with a Tree Pie riding on its back in Rajasthan's Sariska Tiger Reserve. The Nilgai is something of a curiosity: it has none of the grace of the antelopes to which it is related. Instead, it is ungainly, with too small a head and sloping haunches. Its rudimentary horns are bent forward and it runs awkwardly, like a Giraffe, with its head held high. Because of its somewhat cow-like appearance, it is protected by Hindus, and sportsmen disdain shooting it.

Right centre: A female Nilgai with two young. The females are more cow-like than the males.

Below: A group of Red-vented Bulbuls hesitantly slake their thirst.

Below right: A Little Brown Dove drinks at a water hole.

Below: The largest crane in India is the crimson-headed Sarus. When standing erect it is as tall as a man. It is noted for its loud trumpeting calls and elaborate courtship, which involves much leaping, bowing and prancing. In India it is venerated as a symbol of fidelity and family unity because it pairs for life.

Below left: A herd of Nilgai sheltering from the sun under *Phoenix dactalifera* palms in the Sariska Reserve.

Below right: The flower of *Capparis decidua*.

133

Rhesus Macaque monkeys in the Sariska Macaque Reserve. These familiar animals are seen throughout the northern half of India, and are never molested by humans. They are easily distinguished from other species by their orange-red bottoms. Large numbers occur in towns and villages, railway stations and temples, where they beg for food or steal it from wayside stalls. In the wild they prefer roadsides and the edges of forests, and spend more time on the ground than most other monkey species. Those in the Himalaya region have thicker fur, and have been seen at altitudes of up to 2500 metres. In the hotter regions they dive and swim strongly in canals and water tanks. Great numbers were once exported to the United States and Europe – particularly from Bangladesh – for medical research purposes. However, exports are now controlled.

Right and far right: 'The Peacock is the glory of God,' says an early Sanskrit document. These beautiful birds are numerous in India and Pakistan. They were chosen as the 'national bird of India', and they certainly provide a splendid spectacle as they fly about in the Himalayan foothills, or over wildlife reserves. The long, eyed feathers of the males' trains are carefully collected and sold in the village markets for making fans or temple decorations.

Below: A Sambar hind at a water hole in Sariska.

Bottom centre: *Sterculia* trees in flower.

Above: Pythons are India's largest snakes, some growing to a
length of seven metres and capable of crushing prey up to the
size of a small deer in their powerful coils.

Right: Wild Pigs, which are related to the European Wild Boar, cause great losses to Indian farmers, and are almost impossible to keep away from crops. They are the most common prey of Tigers, and in areas where these large predators have disappeared, farmers soon learn – largely through the dramatic increase in the pig population – how crucial a role was played by the Tigers.

Above and right: Chital Deer at a waterhole in the Sariska reserve. The very long antlers of a full-grown stag are illustrated in the picture on the right. These beautiful deer usually move about in herds of 20 to 30, but occasionally build up to 100 or more, with several stags in attendance. Although preyed upon constantly by Tigers, Leopards and Dholes, they breed freely and their numbers in wildlife reserves are increasing.

Top right: Langurs drinking.

Right: A pair of Chinkara Gazelles in the Ranthambhor Reserve in Rajasthan. Small numbers of these gazelles still inhabit the dry areas of north-western India and parts of the Deccan plateau. They are slender and extremely agile animals, capable of short bursts of very high speed when chased by a predator. They can go for long periods without water, obtaining all they need from the dry desert vegetation.

Below: The dragonfly *Brachythemis contaminata*.

Above: A White-necked Stork, a Peacock and several vultures with a herd of Chital Deer in the Ranthambhor Reserve. Such mixed gatherings are frequent at water-holes on the edges of forests – particularly at dawn and dusk, when the big cats lie in wait in the undergrowth to pick off the unwary coming to drink.

Left: A large monitor lizard, the Common Indian Monitor *Varanus bengalensis*, investigates a hollow tree in the reserve.

Far left: A Pond Heron, or Paddy-bird, on the lily *Nymphoides indica*. Paddy-birds are almost as common as Cattle Egrets around rice fields. When they fly, their appearance is transformed by their snow-white wings.

Above left: The inquisitive Jungle Babbler is typical of the many species of this family of birds in India, some of which are fine songsters. It is noisy and very active, moving about in the undergrowth in small, busy groups. This has earned it the Hindi name of *Satbhai*, meaning seven sisters.

Top, above and far right: Ranthambhor has a large population of graceful black-faced Langur monkeys in the forested areas. They live in large troops and feed on flowers, fruit and leaves.

Right: The bole of a Banyan tree, a member of the ubiquitous fig family, showing the mass of roots which descend from it branches, enabling it to spread over a great area. One tree still growing in the Botanic Gardens in Calcutta, and known to have been planted as a seed in 1782, has a circumference of over 420 metres.

Right: Sambar hinds, each with a Black Drongo on its back picking off skin parasites.

Below: In hot weather, Sambar spend most of their time in or near water, taking frequent mud-baths to cool themselves and alleviate the torment of flies.

Bottom: Mature Sambar stags with the shaggy mane and heavy antlers characteristic of the species.

Above: The butterfly *Precis hierta*.

Left: The commensal relationship between birds and deer is again illustrated by this Sambar hind in Ranthambhor, which is closely followed by a Great White Egret and a Grey Heron. The birds snap up insects and frogs disturbed by the hind's progress through the marsh. Even Rhinoceroses are followed in this manner.

Left: Leopards have survived better in India than Tigers because they are more adaptable to changing conditions. The reduction of forests has driven many of them to living near villages, where they prey on domestic animals such as goats, donkeys and poultry. There are stories of Leopards boldly snatching pet dogs from verandahs while the owners sit nearby. Being expert tree climbers, they kill many monkeys, and will carry a deer or a wild pig up into the branches to eat it at leisure. Like Tigers, their role in the ecology of the forest is a positive one because they cull the weak or sickly animals and help to control the population of those which are too numerous.

Above: A Common Tiger butterfly, *Danaus genutia*.

Top left: A King Vulture.

Top right: A Tigress in Ranthambhor Tiger Reserve.

Left: A Jungle Cat in the Ranthambhor Reserve.

Talchhappar Blackbuck Reserve in Rajasthan was specially set up to protect one of the most striking and agile of India's animals. The Blackbuck is the only true antelope in the subcontinent. Excessive hunting very nearly exterminated this animal but fortunately some of the herds kept by the Maharajahs enabled the species to survive. It is now strictly protected in places such as Talchhappar and the Dharwa and Guda Reserves near Jodhpur, where the local Bishnoi people have traditionally protected it. There are other special Blackbuck sanctuaries at Velavadar in Gujarat and at Ranebennur in Karnataka.

Right: Blackbuck females with a young male and two mature males. Talchhappar.

In Pakistan, Blackbuck were virtually exterminated by the 1950s, but with the help of the World Wildlife Fund, they have been restored to the Lal Suhanra reserve. Stocks were obtained from India and from a ranch in Texas, where the species was introduced some years ago, and is now thriving.

Far left and above: Blackbuck are very elegant animals, the males having long spiral horns and handsome, almost black-and-white coats. During the rut they adopt a curious mincing gait, with their heads held almost vertically, while maintaining a long series of grunting notes. They fight vigorously for control of the females.

Left: When alarmed, Blackbuck take off in a series of high leaps, like African Impalas, before breaking into a swift gallop. In the old days, the Maharajahs used to enjoy the sport of having them hunted by Cheetahs, but these animals are now extinct in India.

Right: Half a dozen species of vulture are found in India. This group, photographed after a feast, consists of Long-billed, White-backed and King Vultures.

Above: The much smaller Egyptian Vulture, two of which also appear at the edge of the group far left.

Far left and top: It took these birds some twenty minutes to pick the body of a dead cow to bare bones. The hungry village pie-dog joined the crowd to take advantage of a hasty meal.

Left: After feasting on this carcass, the vultures were unable to fly. Instead, they stood around digesting their meal before taking off like over-laden aircraft.

Right and far right: Bar-headed Geese are migrants to India, crossing the Himalayas from central Asia to reach their winter feeding grounds in reserves such as the Dharwa Lake and Bharatpur.

Bottom right: A flock of beautiful Demoiselle Cranes, which are also migratory. They suffer considerable losses from hunters who sling weighted cords into their passing flocks in Afghanistan and Pakistan.

Below: the fruit of the shrub *Capparis decidua*.

Above: A Demoiselle Crane with a broken wing, probably caused by flying into an overhead power line.

Right: The Desert National Park in the great Thar Desert in Rajasthan is a hostile region with extremely high temperatures. However, it is scenically beautiful where the prevailing winds pile up the sand into Sahara-like dunes. Rain may not fall for a year or more, yet in this harsh environment wildlife still thrives, each species in an elaborate ecosystem which has evolved to take advantage of the available resources. In the absence of rain, dew is drunk from the tips of the sparse grasses, and plants find moisture by thrusting their roots metres-deep into the ground. Many plants are highly specialized. Even mushrooms grow where daytime temperatures can exceed 45°C. A host of strange beetles, lizards, skinks and snakes live on or beneath the surface of the sand. Hardy Desert Hares and Gerbils find shelter in the brittle vegetation, where they are preyed upon by Jackals, Desert Foxes, Desert Cats and a host of birds of prey.

Far right: The wild melon *Citrullus colocynthis*. When ripe, the round fruit is bowled far across the desert by the wind, thus enabling it to disperse its seed.

Right: A *tenebrionid* beetle leaves its track across the desert sand.

Below: Three of the now extremely rare Great Indian Bustards. These large and stately birds are greatly endangered by the steady encroachment of cultivation into the undisturbed grasslands which are their habitat. Serious losses have also been caused by poachers who shoot them from jeeps or from slow-moving bullock carts, to which the bustards pay little attention. The bustards are strictly protected in the Jaisalmer Desert National Park and some other reserves, such as the Bustard Sanctuaries at Ghatigaon and Karera in Madhya Pradesh, but their numbers are still critically small. They used to be plentiful as far south as the plains of the Deccan, where (in 1829) a sportsman once boasted that he had shot 961 of them. They are now found chiefly in a few parts of Rajasthan and Gujarat, some birds occasionally straying across the frontier into Pakistan. Their large eggs, laid on bare ground, are constantly preyed upon by House Crows and Civets. They have an elaborate courtship, the males leaping into the air, rapidly fanning their tails over their backs and inflating their throat-pouches until they hang down between their legs like wobbling balloons.

Top: Winter at the edge of the Thar Desert, with a Laggar Falcon at its roost on a thorn-tree.

Far right: A desert plant, *Calotropis procera*.

Right: Flowering clumps of the desert grass *Eragrostris plumosa*.

157

Above: The Kumbhalgarh Reserve is in a part of
Rajasthan where the scenery changes dramatically.
The desert here gives way to huge outcrops of
eroded basaltic or granitic rocks and deep gorges.

Top right: *Euphorbia* bushes and (in the winter) a profusion
of Cassia spread a colourful canopy across the dry plain.

Middle: The yellow *Cassia auriculata*.

Above: In this area, desert species make way for
moisture-loving creatures such as this stout Ground Boa.

Right: As soon as trees begin to appear, the familiar
Grey Langurs can be heard chattering – and the transition
from desert to almost temperate forest is complete.

Below: Perhaps the bleakest, dustiest and hottest region in India is the Great Rann of Kutch. It stretches for hundreds of square kilometres in the State of Gujarat, from the frontier with Pakistan's Sind desert, southward to the Little Rann and the Gulf of Kutch. It is a desolate area of unrelieved, sun-baked saline clay desert, shimmering with the images of a perpetual mirage.

Above and right: The Little Rann is the last refuge of the Indian Wild Ass, an exceptionally hardy animal which contrives to live and even breed in this harsh environment, feeding on the withered grass which grows in the depressions. There were once many thousands of Wild Asses roaming the dry plains of India, but their numbers and their range have steadily declined until today barely 2000 remain. They are no longer hunted, although poachers kill a few and soldiers (this is a sensitive frontier region) sometimes harass them by chasing them in jeeps. The present decline was caused mainly by diseases introduced by domestic cattle.

Left: A pair of Pied Kingfishers.

Below left: A profusion of white flowers against a rich blue sky.

Below: *Cassia fistula*.

Top left: The Gir Forest National Park in Gujarat, now one of the most important in India, was once the property of the Nawabs of Junagadh. It was over-run by land-hungry villagers after the Partition of India. The forest was the last refuge of the Asiatic Lion, of which there were still about 300 in 1955. With the loss of vegetation, the deer on which the Lions fed soon disappeared, and they began to starve. By 1969, only 177 survived. The Gujarat State then turned the forest into a protected reserve and re-settled the villagers elsewhere. The vegetation recovered, the deer returned, and today they are thriving. The Lions have sufficient prey, with the result that their numbers have increased to around 217.

Far left: The colouring of these Painted Sandgrouse hens merges with the forest floor to provide a fine camouflage.

Left: The more brightly coloured Painted Sandgrouse cock, whose plumage earns the species its name.

The Gir Lions are the Asiatic, forest-loving relatives of the African Lion. Their range once extended from Greece to central India, but those in the Gir are the last survivors – of which India is rightly proud. The National Park is one of the best-managed in the country, and provides good facilities for visitors to see these unique animals in their forest habitat.

Overleaf: A fine pride of Lions in the Gir National Park.

164

The Deccan
The Southern Tableland of India

In the days of conquest, before roads and railways physically unified India, the great triangular southern peninsula was almost a different world, divided from the Indo-Gangetic plain, from east to west, by the scattered ranges of the Vindhya Mountains. These are neither very high nor quite continuous, but in the early days were linked in the valleys by hostile jungle which discouraged penetration. Today the barrier effect is less evident, but geographically the difference between north and south of the Vindhyas remains self-evident.

Instead of the endless flat plain, little above sea level, the Deccan peninsula is based on raised granitic rock. In the north-west, in what geologists call the Deccan trap, are extensive outflows of ancient basaltic lava, capped more recently with laterite. Down either side of the peninsula, like sea-walls, run the long ranges of the Western and Eastern Ghats. Their average elevations are respectively about 1000 and 500 metres, with here and there peaks rising to twice or three times as high. They merge at the southern tip of the triangle to form the plateau of the beautiful Nilgiri Hills, with the Dodabetta peak triumphantly marking the junction.

The Western Ghats rise abruptly almost from the sea as an unbroken challenge to the south-west monsoon. The high rainfall on their seaward slopes produces a heavy cladding of luxurious rain-forest. From their eastern flanks flow fast-running rivers, some of which, such as the Godavari, the Cauvery and the Kistna, traverse the whole tableland, winding through the minor inland mountains to drain by the valleys through the Eastern Ghats into the Bay of Bengal. The less spectacular Eastern Ghats do not hug the shore but are fragmented, leaving coastal lowlands before resuming their southward course. They too are forested, but the vegetation is less lush than on their western counterparts. Here, in southern India, the high mountain slopes and forests of the Nilgiris have similar species to those of the Assam ranges – including a distinctive Tahr, (wild goat) and a Langur monkey. Sal woodlands to the north give way to teak and semi-evergreen tropical forest in the south. Throughout the southern peninsula scenery is far more varied and dramatic than in the Indo-Gangetic Plain. The industrious people of southern India are also more varied than their northern neighbours and maintain many colourful traditions and religious festivals.

The inland hill regions often enjoy a delightful climate and are of surpassing beauty. In the days of the British raj places such as Ootacamund were often preferred to Kashmir or Darjeeling as hot-weather retreats. Elegant houses with names such as 'Journey's End' or 'Rose Cottage' were built there, each with a traditional English garden, full of such favourites as Delphiniums and Marguerites, but now quietly being reclaimed by the jungle.

Wildlife is abundant in the less accessible parts of the Deccan and many splendid Reserves and National Parks have been established. Tigers and their prey species are thriving in the teak and bamboo forests. In the south they can be seen in the Bandipur Tiger Reserve in Karnataka and in the tropical evergreen jungle of Periyar in Kerala. The rare and very striking Lion-tailed Macaque monkey has its last refuge in the rain-forests of the Western Ghats, and some 6000 wild Elephants still roam the dense forests at the convergence of the States of Karnataka, Kerala and Tamil Nadu.

In the wildlife reserves particular attention is now paid to maintaining freshwater pools and streams, most of which would normally run dry in the hot season. It is to them that wildlife must come to drink and bathe. An observation post near one of them is one of the best ways of seeing Tigers, Elephants and various deer during the summer months.

Crocodiles and several species of big sea turtles have special reserves on the coasts of the peninsula and vast numbers of various wading birds abound near all of the picturesque fishing villages. Even around the great coastal cities, such as Bombay and Madras, a considerable variety of wildlife lives in parks and gardens. Throughout the region, peninsula India provides a breath-taking abundance of colour, variety and interest for the naturalist.

A coastal scene in Goa, on the west coast of India. This was once a Portuguese colony.

Right: A coastal forest of Toddy Palms, *Borassus flabellifer* near Madras.

Below: Vine snakes or Common Green Whip Snakes (*Ahaetulla nasuta*) with a Bronzeback Tree Snake, *Dendrelaphis sp.*

Bottom left: Fallen fruit of the Toddy Palm.

Bottom right: The Indian Chameleon (*Chamaeleo zeylanicus*).

Right: The Great White Egret is the largest of the four egret species in India. In the breeding season, the upper parts of its black legs are flushed with orange and the skin at the base of its bill turns bright blue. Like the other egrets, it erects the long scapular feathers on its back during courtship to form a delicate white cloak.

Above: A Cattle Egret in full breeding plumage.

Above left: Fox Bats roosting in a tree in the Reserve.

Left: A colony of Indian Cliff Swallows at their bottle-shaped mud nests beside the Cauvery River in the Ranganathittoo Bird Reserve.

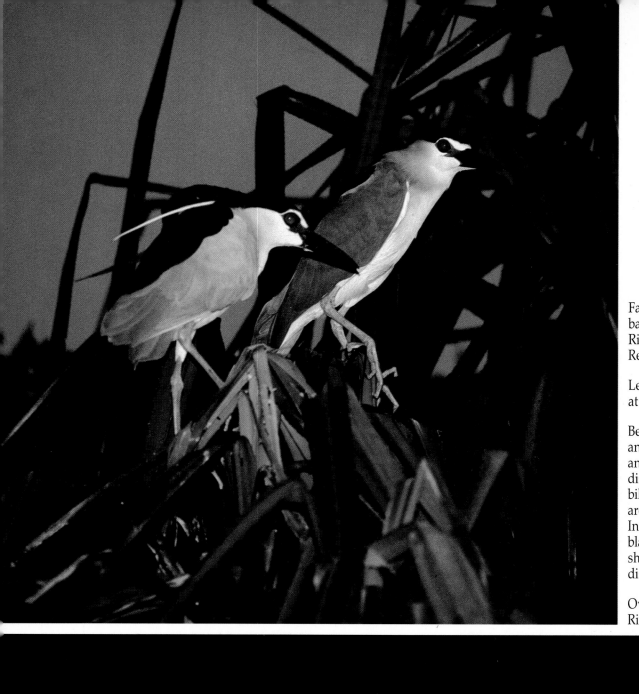

Far left: A Mugger, or Marsh Crocodile, basks on an exposed rock in the Cauvery River in the Ranganathittoo Bird Reserve, Karnataka State.

Left: Colonies of Night Herons nest at Ranganathittoo.

Below: From left to right are a Little Egret, an Openbill Stork, an Intermediate Egret and a Cattle Egret. The Little Egret is distinguished by its small size, fine black bill and black legs with yellow feet (which are here hidden in the mud); the Intermediate Egret has a yellow bill and black legs; the Cattle Egret has a much shorter, flesh-coloured bill and a distinctive, heavy jowl.

Overleaf: A drowned forest in the Kabini River, Karnataka.

Top: Elephants bathing in a *jheel* in the Nagarhole National Park. This park, in Karnataka in the south of the Indian peninsula, is a good place to see elephants in the luxuriant forests and bamboo thickets which they most enjoy. Their total population in southern India is now about 6000, nearly all living in the area where Karnataka, Tamil Nadu and Kerala adjoin in the shadow of the Western Ghats. Efforts are being made to prevent further encroachment on these wonderful forests.

Left: Very old elephants like this solitary old bull with a single tusk, are sometimes separated from the herd.

Bottom left: Indian Shags nest on skeletal trees in the drowned forest on the Kabini River.

Bottom centre: *Panaeolus* – gill-bearing fungi growing on elephant droppings.

Bottom right: An elephant family makes its way through the forest in Nagarhole.

Below: A Brown Fish Owl showing its characteristic yellow eyes and streaked breast.

Above: A fully adult Gaur bull (shown with a pair of Mynahs on its back) would not be attacked by a Tiger, but calves are frequent victims.

Above left: The Nagarhole National Park provides an opportunity to see some of the southern population of Gaur Jungle Bison. The distinctive white feet and the high ridged shoulders of the bulls are shown clearly in this photograph.

Left: A species of parasitic *Cuscuta*, which slowly smothers its host.

Far left: A mating pair of Crimson Rose butterflies, *Pachiliopta hector,* which belong to the swallowtail group.

Centre left: Flowers of an *Aneilema* species.

Above: Three of India's colourful libellulid dragonflies: *Brachythemis contaminata* (top), *Neurothemis tullia* female (middle) and *Neurothemis tullia* male (bottom).

Top: A Sambar stag in the well-forested Bandipur Tiger Reserve in Karnataka.

Above: Grey Junglefowl are widespread in southern India. This cock and hen were feeding at a termite nest, deftly catching the 'flying ants' as they emerged.

Right: A winged population of termites, *Odontotermes sp.*, emerges from their nest to create a new colony elsewhere.

Peafowl are common in the Bandipur Reserve. Like the Langur monkeys, they are constantly alert to the approach of a Tiger or Leopard, and their screaming alarm cries save many a deer or wild pig from being caught. The peafowl on the right, with the damaged train, may have been attacked by a Leopard. These predators often try to catch peafowl at water-holes and, if inexperienced, sometimes pounce on the long train rather than the bird. When moulting, the feathers of the train are dropped singly. The tail beneath them is quite short.

Right: A group of Chital hinds in a grassy forest glade in the Mudumalai Tiger Reserve in Tamil Nadu.

Far right top: An adult male Chital calls to his hinds.

Far right centre: As the rutting season approaches, a Chital stag rubs its antlers against the back of a tree to cleanse them of remnants of 'velvet'.

Right: The tiny Mouse Deer, or Chevrotain, is not much larger than a hare. Unlike true deer, this defenseless creature has four toes to each foot, and no antlers. It occurs in the forested hills of southern India up to an elevation of about 1800 metres.

Centre right: A Spotted Owlet with a beetle it has just caught.

Bottom right: Well-camouflaged nestlings of the Red-wattled Lapwing.

Far right bottom: The flowers of a species of *Curcuma*.

Above: A colony of *Vespidae* social wasps on the surface of their paper nest.

Top: The forest is the habitat of the Nilgiri Langur, distinguished by its copious pale face ruffle.

Left: The rich, moist, deciduous forest of Mudumalai Reserve gives way in the south to the scrub vegetation of the Nilgiri Hills range.

Bonnet Macaque monkeys in the Mudumalai Reserve in Tamil Nadu. They are easily recognised by the untidy 'bonnets' of long hair radiating from their crowns. They are fairly numerous in southern India south of the Godavari River. Like the Rhesus Macaque in the north, they are usually very tame, and occupy most towns and villages, where they have an annoying and widespread habit of removing the tiles from roofs – perhaps in a search for insects. Many are trained by street beggars to perform tricks.

Right and below: There are many
distinctive varieties of the handsome
Indian Giant Squirrel. The variety found
in the moist evergreen forests of the
Malabar coastal region is black above
and bright reddish-orange below, whereas
the race in the dry deciduous forests at
the northern end of the Western Ghats is
a pale sandy colour. These large
squirrels (two and a half times larger
than European squirrels) spend most
of their lives among the higher branches,
and are difficult to observe closely.
The squirrel on the right is feeding on
the flowers of a *Terminalia crenulata*
in the Mudumalai Reserve.

Above: By skilful management, the pools and streams in the Mudumalai Reserve have become perennial, to the great benefit of the wildlife. The trees are no longer lopped for firewood and beautiful scenes such as the one above are now common.

Centre left: An Indian Giant Squirrel.

Left: A male *Calotes* lizard displaying its inflated throat as a warning to rivals.

Left: The Moyar Gorge in the Nilgiri Hills is typical of the magnificent scenery of the southern region of the Indian peninsula.

Top: The delicate flowers of *Rhodomyrtus parviflora*.

Above: Many species of lizard, such as this yellow-necked Rock Lizard, *Psammophilus dorsalis*, inhabit the rocky gorges of the Nilgiri Hills.

Overleaf: The granitic crags of the Western Ghats rise dramatically from the edge of the plain.

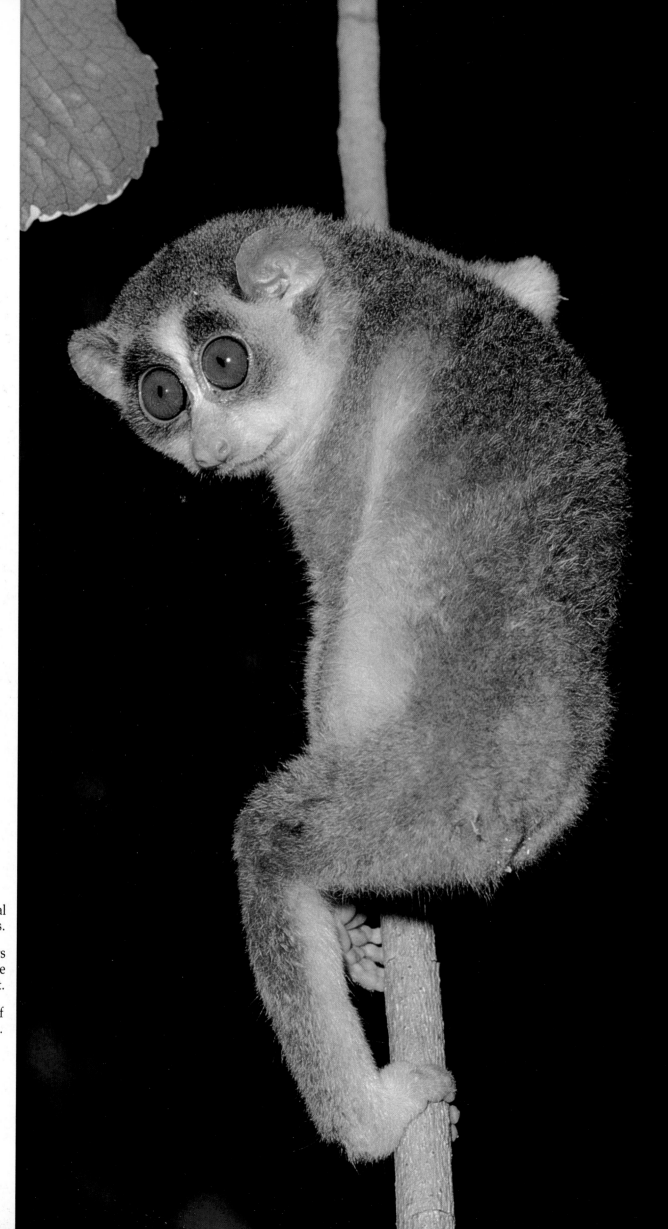

Right: A nocturnal
Slender Loris.

Bottom left: Flowers
of *Cassia fistula* in the
Anaimalai forest.

Bottom right: Flowers of
an orange *Mussaenda sp*.

Left: A pair of Large Southern Golden-backed Woodpeckers. Note the chips flying as the upper bird 'drills' into the branch.

Below: A Sloth Bear beside its lair.

Right: A one-tusked elephant bull emerges from thick forest in Anaimalai's Karian *shola*.

Above: In the *shola* evergreen forest of the Anaimalai Sanctuary, the rare Lion-tailed Macaque monkeys still maintain a stronghold. They can be found elsewhere only in the rain forests of the Ashambu Hills of the Western Ghats, and the Nellcampathi Hills in Kerala. Their shiny black fur, long, lion-like manes and tufted tails make them instantly recognizable. Only a few hundred remain, and these monkeys are listed as a gravely endangered species.

Left: A forested landscape in the Anaimalai Hills, which form part of the western Ghats.

197

Above: The Kerala
Highlands near Munnar.

Right: The orchid
Dendrobium nanum.

198

Above: The Rajamalai Sanctuary in the Kerala Highlands is the home of the Nilgiri Tahr. These shy, sure-footed wild goats are restricted to the stony scarps at elevations of 1200 to 1850 metres. Slightly smaller than their Himalayan relatives, they have shorter, darker fur which in the older males is almost black, with a distinctive white saddle-patch across the loins.

Left: The purple flowering *Aristea ecklonii*, recorded for the first time in India, at an altitude of about 2000 metres in the Rajamalai Sanctuary.

Above: Like all wild goats, Nilgiri Tahrs have exceptionally keen eyesight, and can be approached only after arduous stalking across the barren slopes where they feed. During the heat of the day, they lie hidden among the rocks or higher levels, descending the slopes in the cool of dawn or evening. Their main enemy is the Leopard, which stalks them with great skill. Although their meat is not very palatable to humans, tahrs were once hunted. Today, however, they are well protected in the Kerala Highlands. All the other species of wild goats are restricted to northern India, and it is thought that the Nilgiri Tahr may have evolved from a population isolated by climatic changes which occurred many millions of years ago.

Top left: The buttress roots of a climbing fig.

Top right: Turtles bask on the bank of the Periyar River in the Periyar Tiger Reserve.

Above: A colourful Dragonfly, *Trithemis aurora*.

Left: A predatory spider which has just caught a libellulid dragonfly, *Neurothemis tullia,* begins its meal by sucking the juices from the insect's head.

201

Far right: The Periyar Tiger Reserve is not large – only 777 square kilometres including its protective buffer zone – but it is important as it has plenty of water – especially from the dammed river. The Reserve is famous in southern India for its elephant herds, the activities of which can often be observed on the grassy shores of the huge lake. Sadly, relentless poaching has taken a heavy toll of the male tuskers', and today these are rarely seen. Periyar also embraces some of the finest tracts of undamaged wet-evergreen and semi-evergreen forest in southern India.

Top: Large numbers of deer, such as this Sambar herd, feed on the marshy borders of the lake in the Periyar Reserve, providing good prey for Tigers.

Above: Nilgiri Langurs are also numerous. Their black colouring, white ruffles and exceptionally long tails distinguish them from the Common Langur.

Overleaf: A palm-fringed shore at the southern tip of the Indian subcontinent.

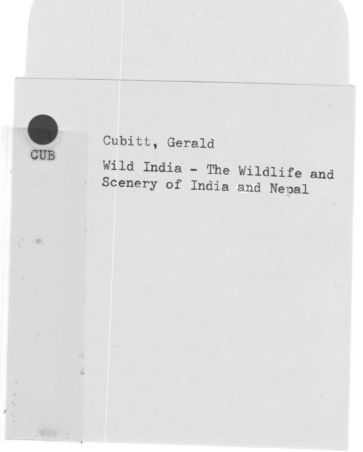

Cubitt, Gerald

Wild India - The Wildlife and
Scenery of India and Nepal